DH Department of Health

An organisation with a memory

Report of an expert group on learning from adverse events in the NHS

Chaired by the Chief Medical Officer

London
The Stationery Office

First published 2000
Second impression 2000

ISBN 0 11 322441 9

Printed in the United Kingdom for The Stationery Office.
TJ3260 c15   12/00

CONTENTS

FOREWORD

by the Secretary of State for Health

The Government is committed to building a new NHS that offers faster, fairer and higher-quality services to patients. The modern NHS we are creating must be constantly alert to opportunities to review and improve its performance.

Advances in knowledge and technology have in recent decades immeasurably increased the power of health care to do good, to prevent or treat illnesses against which there was previously no defence. Yet they have also immeasurably increased the complexity of health care systems. Their unique combination of processes, technologies and human interactions means that modern health care systems are among the most complex in the world.

With that complexity comes an inevitable risk that at times things will go wrong. And in health care when things go wrong the stakes are higher than in almost any other sphere of human activity.

No-one pretends that adverse health care events, as this report has termed them, can be eliminated from modern health care. Health care interventions usually bring great benefits, but they can sometimes cause harm if things go wrong. The challenge is to ensure that the modern NHS is as safe a place as possible for patients, and that the outcomes of its care are skewed even more overwhelmingly to the positive. That is a challenge this Government is determined to meet.

Too often in the past we have witnessed tragedies which could have been avoided had the lessons of past experience been properly learned. The task of the Expert Group was to advise the Government on the steps that can be taken to ensure that the NHS learns from its experiences, so that the risk of avoidable harm to patients is minimised.

This report examines the key factors at work in organisational failure and learning, a range of practical experience from other sectors and the present state of learning mechanisms in the NHS before drawing conclusions and making recommendations. Its recommendations include the creation of a new national system for reporting and analysing adverse health care events, to make sure that key lessons are identified and learned, along with other measures to support work at local level to analyse events and learn the lessons when things go wrong.

I welcome this report and will be studying its findings very closely. My fellow Ministers and I will be working with the Chief Medical Officer over the next few months to decide how best to take forward the necessary action.

Alan Milburn
Secretary of State for Health

EXECUTIVE SUMMARY

1   The great majority of NHS care is of a very high clinical standard, and serious failures are uncommon in relation to the high volume of care provided every day in hospitals and in the community. Yet where serious failures in care do occur they can have devastating consequences for individual patients and their families, cause distress to the usually very committed health care staff involved and undermine public confidence in the services the NHS provides. In addition, the cumulative financial cost of adverse events to the NHS and to the economy is huge. Most distressing of all, such failures often have a familiar ring, displaying strong similarities to incidents which have occurred before and in some cases almost exactly replicating them. Many could be avoided if only the lessons of experience were properly learned.

2   The introduction of clinical governance provides NHS organisations with a powerful imperative to focus on tackling adverse health care events. This report, commissioned by Health Ministers from an expert group under the chairmanship of the Chief Medical Officer, sets out to review what we know about the scale and nature of serious failures in NHS health care, to examine the extent to which the NHS has the capacity to learn from such failures when they do occur and to recommend measures which could help to ensure that the likelihood of repeated failures is minimised in the future. The work of the group was informed by evidence and experience from a range of sectors other than health, including industry, aviation and academic research.

The problem

3   Currently, NHS reporting and information systems provide us with a patchy and incomplete picture of the scale and nature of the problem of serious failures in health care. We know, for example, that every year:

- 400 people die or are seriously injured in adverse events involving medical devices;
- nearly 10,000 people are reported to have experienced serious adverse reactions to drugs;
- around 1,150 people who have been in recent contact with mental health services commit suicide;

- nearly 28,000 written complaints are made about aspects of clinical treatment in hospitals;

- the NHS pays out around £400 million a year settlement of clinical negligence claims, and has a potential liability of around £2.4 billion for existing and expected claims;

- hospital acquired infections – around 15% of which may be avoidable – are estimated to cost the NHS nearly £1 billion.

4   Just as none of these statistics can be attributed wholly to service failures, research in this country and abroad suggests that they give no indication of the potential true scale of the problem. This issue has been the subject of major pieces of academic research in Australia and the USA, but work in the UK is in its infancy. Yet the best research-based estimates we have reveal enough to suggest that in NHS hospitals alone adverse events in which harm is caused to patients:

- occur in around 10% of admissions – or at a rate in excess of 850,000 a year;

- cost the service an estimated £2 billion a year in additional hospital stays alone, without taking any account of human or wider economic costs.

5   In addition, there is evidence that some specific types of relatively infrequent but very serious adverse events happen time and again over a period of years. Inquiries and incident investigations determine that 'the lessons must be learned', but the evidence suggests that the NHS as a whole is not good at doing so. Still less is known about the situation in primary care, despite the fact that it accounts for the great majority of NHS patient contacts and can still experience service failures which have serious consequences for individual patients.

Evidence and experience

6   Research on learning from failures in health care is relatively sparse, yet the evidence from other areas of activity – and in particular from industry – reveals a rich seam of valuable knowledge about the nature of failure and of learning which is as relevant to health care as to any other area of human activity.

7   When things go wrong, whether in health care or in another environment, the response has often been an attempt to identify an individual or individuals who must carry the blame. The focus of incident analysis has tended to be on the events immediately surrounding an adverse event, and in particular on the human acts or omissions immediately preceding the event itself.

8   It is of course right, in health care as in any other field, that individuals must sometimes be held to account for their actions – in particular if there is evidence of gross negligence or recklessness, or of criminal behaviour. Yet in

the great majority of cases, the causes of serious failures stretch far beyond the actions of the individuals immediately involved. Safety is a dynamic, not a static situation. In a socially and technically complex field such as health care, a huge number of factors are at work at any one time which influence the likelihood of failure. These factors are a combination of:

- **active failures**: 'unsafe acts' committed by those working at the sharp end of a system, which are usually short-lived and often unpredictable; and

- **latent conditions**: that can develop over time and lie dormant before combining with other factors or active failures to breach a system's safety defences. They are long-lived and, unlike many active failures, can be identified and removed before they cause an adverse event.

9   Human error may sometimes be the factor that immediately precipitates a serious failure, but there are usually deeper, systemic factors at work which if addressed would have prevented the error or acted as a safety-net to mitigate its consequences. We illustrate this point with case studies from the NHS and from many other sectors, including the aviation industry.

10   Activity to learn from and prevent failures therefore needs to address their wider causes. It also needs to stretch beyond simply diagnosing and publicising the lessons from incidents, to ensure that these lessons are embedded in practice. The distinction between passive learning (where lessons are identified but not put into practice) and active learning (where those lessons are embedded into an organisation's culture and practices) is crucial in under-standing why truly effective learning so often fails to take place.

11   It is possible to identify a number of barriers that can prevent active learning from taking place, but there are two areas in particular where the NHS can draw valuable lessons from the experience of other sectors.

- **Organisational culture** is central to every stage of the learning process – from ensuring that incidents are identified and reported through to embedding the necessary changes deeply into practice. There is evidence that 'safety cultures', where open reporting and balanced analysis are encouraged in principle and by example, can have a positive and quantifiable impact on the performance of organisations. 'Blame cultures' on the other hand can encourage people to cover up errors for fear of retribution and act against the identification of the true causes of failure, because they focus heavily on individual actions and largely ignore the role of underlying systems. The culture of the NHS still errs too much towards the latter;

- **Reporting systems** are vital in providing a core of sound, representative information on which to base analysis and recommendations. Experience in other sectors demonstrates the value of systematic approaches to recording and reporting adverse events and the merits of quarrying information on 'near misses' as well as events which actually result in harm. The NHS does not compare well with best practice in either of these areas.

12   Despite the particular characteristics and complexities of health care systems, there is much of value that can be gleaned from research and wider experience about the nature of both failure and learning. The experience of other sectors provides valuable pointers towards ways in which NHS systems might be developed.

NHS systems for learning from failure

13   A number of systems already exist in the NHS which can, to varying extents, be seen as mechanisms for learning from adverse health care events, but collectively they have serious limitations. These NHS systems include:

- a number of local, regional and national incident reporting schemes;
- ongoing national studies in specific areas of care, such as the four Confidential Inquiries;
- systems, such as those for complaints and litigation, which are designed to investigate or respond to specific instances of poor quality care;
- periodic external studies and reviews (e.g. the Audit Commission's Value for Money studies);
- health and public health statistics; and
- a range of internal and external incident inquiries.

14   Some of these systems (such as the Confidential Inquiries and the national reporting system for incidents involving medical devices) achieve good coverage of very specific categories of event, and produce high-quality recommendations based on analysis of the information collected. Overall though coverage is patchy and there are many gaps. Guidance on the reporting of adverse incidents in the NHS stretches back over 40 years, but there is still no standardised reporting system, nor indeed a standard definition of what should be reported.

15   Local risk reporting systems, which should provide a bedrock for onward reporting to regional or national systems, are developing but similarly variable. Incident reporting systems appear to be particularly poorly-developed in primary care, and systematic reporting of 'near misses' (seen as an important early warning of serious problems) is almost non-existent across the NHS.

16   Systems vary too in the degree to which the information collected is subject to analysis with the aim of promoting learning. Information from the complaints system and from health care litigation in particular appear to be greatly under-exploited as a learning resource. The NHS also secures variable value, both financially and in useful learning extracted, from the range of ad hoc incident investigations and inquiries undertaken every year. There is no single focal point for NHS information on adverse events, and at present it is spread across nearly 1.000 different organisations.

17   The NHS record in implementing the recommendations that emerge from these various systems is patchy. Too often lessons are identified but true 'active' learning does not take place because the necessary changes are not properly embedded in practice. Though there is some good evidence of meaningful medium and long-term change as a result of Confidential Inquiry recommendations, for example, these are rarely driven through into practice and the onus for implementation and prioritisation is very much on local services. Takeup can tend to 'plateau' once changes have been implemented by those who are most naturally receptive to them, and there is some evidence that progress nationally can slip back if efforts are not sustained.

18   The renewed focus on quality as a core component of the Government's NHS modernisation programme provides an opportunity to address some of these shortcomings. The reporting and analysis of adverse health care events should be a specific focus for action, over and above the general drive for improved risk management and better risk reporting.

The Way Forward

19   The time is right for a fundamental re-thinking of the way that the NHS approaches the challenge of learning from adverse health care events. The NHS often fails to learn the lessons when things go wrong, and has an old-fashioned approach in this area compared to some other sectors. Yet the potential benefits of modernisation are tremendous – in terms of lives saved, harm prevented and resources freed up for the delivery of more and better care.

20   We believe that, if the NHS is successfully to modernise its approach to learning from failure, there are four key areas that must be addressed. In summary, the NHS needs to develop:
   ● unified mechanisms for reporting and analysis when things go wrong;
   ● a more open culture, in which errors or service failures can be reported and discussed;
   ● mechanisms for ensuring that, where lessons are identified, the necessary changes are put into practice;
   ● a much wider appreciation of the value of the system approach in preventing, analysing and learning from errors.

21   Only if these four conditions are met can the NHS hope to develop the modern and effective approach to learning from failures that it so badly needs. It is the specific action needed to create these conditions that our conclusions and recommendations seek to address in detail.

GLOSSARY

Throughout this report we use a number of terms the definition of which has been the subject of much debate. An accurate appreciation of the meaning attached to these terms is important in understanding fully our report and its conclusions. This brief glossary sets out the meanings we have attributed to these key terms in our report.

Adverse health care event
An event or omission arising during clinical care and causing physical or psychological injury to a patient

Error
The failure to complete a planned action as intended, or the use of an incorrect plan of action to achieve a given aim[1]

Hazard
Anything that can cause harm[2]

Health care near miss
A situation in which an event or omission, or a sequence of events or omissions, arising during clinical care fails to develop further, whether or not as the result of compensating action, thus preventing injury to a patient

Risk
The likelihood, high or low, that somebody or something will be harmed by a hazard, multiplied by the severity of the potential harm

System
A set of interdependent elements interacting to achieve a common aim. These elements may be both human and non-human (equipment, technologies etc.).[3]

ACKNOWLEDGEMENTS

The Committee is indebted to a number of individuals and organisations who have helped with its work. In particular, thanks are due to Dr P Jane Cowan (Medico-legal Advisor, Medical Protection Society), Dr Maureen Dalziel (formerly Medical Director, NHS Litigation Authority), Mr Gareth Edwards (formerly Principal Consultant, Knowledge Management, BP Amoco), Dr Stephen Green and Dr Christine Tomkins (Medical Defence Union Limited), Ms Amanda Hedley, Ms Anne Easter and Ms Shareen Campbell (East Wiltshire NHS Trust) and Mr Arnold Simanowitz (President, Action for Victims of Medical Accidents). In addition we have received considerable help from a wide range of staff from within the Department of Health and its Agencies, and thanks are due to them also. Any errors of fact and omissions as well as the opinions expressed in the report are our own.

CHAPTER 1

Introduction

In this chapter we set out the rationale for the group's task. Serious incidents and failures of services are uncommon in relation to the high volume of care provided throughout the NHS every day. Yet when they do occur they can have disastrous implications for patients and their families. When we read about serious problems they often have a familiar ring, displaying similarities to incidents which have occurred before. The expert group was set up to examine the extent to which the NHS currently has the capacity to learn from incidents and service failures, and to recommend steps which might be taken to help ensure that similar events can be avoided in the future.

1.1   In December 1997, the Government published a White Paper *The New NHS: Modern, Dependable* [4], which set out a ten year modernisation strategy for the NHS. One of the main aims of the proposals set out in the White Paper is to bring about a major improvement in the quality of clinical care delivered to patients in the NHS.

A programme to improve quality in the NHS

1.2   As part of these changes, a formal responsibility for quality has been placed on every health organisation in the country through arrangements for clinical governance at local level. This responsibility is underpinned by a new statutory duty of quality on NHS providers.

Clinical Governance

"A framework through which NHS organisations are accountable for continuously improving the quality of their services and safeguarding high standards of care by creating an environment in which excellence in clinical care will flourish" [5]

1.3   Clinical governance is thus an organisational concept. It requires the creation of a culture as well as systems and methods of working which will ensure that opportunities for quality improvement are identified in all the organisation's services and that over time there is a major step up in the quality of care provided throughout the NHS.

1.4   Under these new policies local clinical governance is reinforced by new national structures: National Service Frameworks and the National Institute for Clinical Excellence (NICE) will set standards, a new NHS Performance Assessment Framework will provide a better-balanced means of gauging NHS performance and the Commission for Health Improvement (CHI) will review local clinical governance arrangements. The Commission will also have a 'trouble-shooting' role to help individual NHS organisations identify the root causes of serious difficulties and advise on the measures needed to resolve them.

Shifting the quality curve

1.5   If a simple summary measure were available of the quality of care produced by each NHS organisation and each clinical team within that organisation, we might expect that the majority would tend to cluster near the middle of the range. Outlying values, whether representing very good quality or very poor, would be much less common than more 'average' performance. One such pattern is shown in Figure 1.1. The exact form of the curve is not important, only that values towards the middle of the curve are common in comparison with those at the two extremes. This form of central tendency is generally found in complex and biological systems such as those underlying health care delivery.

Figure 1.1:
Variation in the Quality of Organisations

Source: Scally and Donaldson 1998[6]

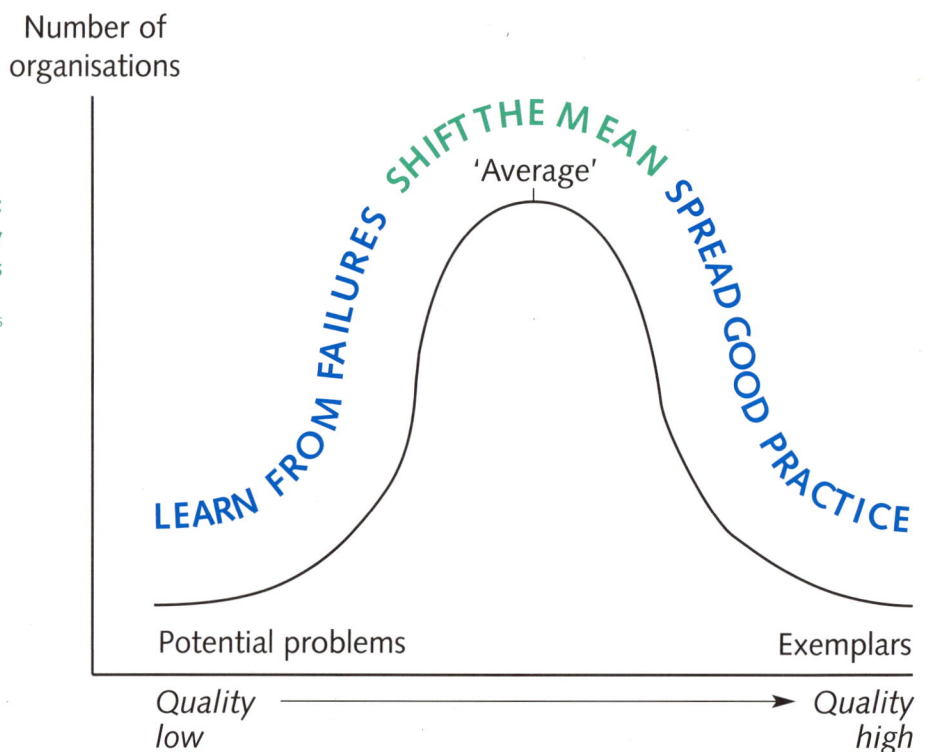

"quality must be 'everybody's business', and not simply an issue for the very best and the very worst"

1.6   The Government's policies for the NHS aim to address all aspects of this quality curve. By doing so, and shifting the curve in Fig. 1.1 to the right in the direction of higher quality, the major benefits will come from improving the position of the 'average', where the bulk of health care organisations and clinical teams lie. This underlies the philosophy that quality must be 'everybody's business', and not simply an issue for the very best and the very worst. This is a key principle of current policy to improve clinical quality within the framework of clinical governance.

1.7   It is also important, though, that we do not lose sight of the left-hand tail of the curve in Fig. 1.1. Organisational performance in the NHS will never be homogenised to the extent that this 'tail' will be altogether eliminated, and it is inevitable that whatever the position of the curve itself there will always be organisations whose performance is worse (or better) than the average. The adverse events and failures which lie behind this part of the curve, however infrequently they may occur, can be a source of valuable learning. They need to be studied so that valid lessons can be drawn, communicated and learned for the benefit of the NHS and its future patients. That process provides the focus for the rest of our report. As a result our report is bound to concentrate disproportionately on instances of poor outcome and failure.

Addressing serious quality problems

1.8   The 'problem' tail of the quality curve has caused greatest concern in recent years. This is for two reasons. Firstly, although serious problems in the quality of health care are uncommon in proportion to the high volume of very good care provided, when they do occur they can have devastating consequences for individuals and their families. Secondly, stories about very poor care regularly hit the headlines and they worry people. They give the impression that the NHS is powerless to prevent such disasters and they generally undermine public confidence in services. Rightly or wrongly, accounts of particular health service failures lead to the perception that they may be only the tip of an iceberg beneath which much more poor quality lies.

1.9   This is an area where the NHS has not had a strong track record over its 52 years of existence. The Government has recently acted to address the problem of unacceptable quality of care arising from the poor clinical performance of doctors. A consultation paper[7] has been published setting out proposals to completely modernise the approach to poor clinical performance, with a much greater emphasis on its prevention and early recognition and on fast, fair and effective resolution of problems when they do occur.

1.10 Not all serious failures in quality of care will be due either wholly or in part to poor performance by a doctor or other health professional. Poor professional performance may occur in conjunction with other problems within the organisation. Alternatively, the service failures may result from human error rather than being the end result of a pattern of poor practitioner performance. Invariably though, human error will be combined with wider organisational factors which contributed to the failure. This, as will become apparent, is one of the major themes of this report.

1.11 Over time, we would expect the development of clinical governance in all health care organisations within the NHS to reduce the likelihood of service failure. An important part of this local process will be the further development of risk management programmes, an approach which is already well underway as part of the overall NHS approach to controls assurance. The work of the Commission for Health Improvement will assist and reinforce these local developments in quality improvement.

An absence of learning from failure

"the NHS is behind some other sectors where there are risks in service delivery and where human safety is at stake"

1.12 Amidst this major and comprehensive range of measures to assure and improve quality in the NHS, there is one remaining weak link. The NHS has no reliable way of identifying serious lapses of standards of care, analysing them systematically, learning from them and introducing change which sticks so as to prevent similar events from recurring. In this respect the NHS is behind some other sectors where there are risks in service delivery and where human safety is at stake.

1.13 There are a number of things we should expect to see if, overall, systems for minimising and learning from failures are working well.

A service working well should expect that:

- Serious failures of standards of care are uncommon.
- Serious failures of a similar kind do not recur on a future occasion.
- Incidents where services have failed in one part of the country are not repeated elsewhere.
- Systems are in place which reduce to a minimum the likelihood of serious failure in standards of care happening.
- Attention is also paid to monitoring and reducing levels of less serious incidents.

1.14 The starting point for this report was that these conditions are by and large not fulfilled at present. Experience suggests that the NHS as a service is not expert at preventing serious incidents or occurrences in which patients are harmed or experience very poor outcomes of care. Nor does it always learn efficiently or effectively from such failures when they do occur.

The present NHS position on adverse incidents

- Some failures occur which are avoidable.
- Untoward events which could be prevented recur, sometimes with devastating consequences.
- Incidents which result in lapses in standards of care in one or more health organisations do not reliably lead to corrections throughout the NHS.
- Circumstances that predispose to failure, and which if addressed could allow risks to be minimised, are not well recognised.

The price of failure

1.15 The importance of addressing this deficit – the failure to learn reliably from adverse events – is illustrated by seven simple facts:

- Research suggests that an estimated 850,000 (range 300,000 to 1.4 million) adverse events might occur each year in the NHS hospital sector, resulting in a £2 billion direct cost in additional hospital days alone; some adverse events will be inevitable complications of treatment but around half might be avoidable.

- The NHS paid out around £400 million[8] in clinical litigation settlements in the financial year 1998/99 and has a potential liability of around £2.4 billion from existing and expected claims; when analysed many cases of litigation show potentially avoidable causes.

- There were over 38,000 complaints about all aspects of Family Health Services during 1998–99, and nearly 28,000 written complaints about aspects of clinical treatment in hospitals alone[9].

- At least 13 patients have died or been paralysed since 1985 because a drug has been wrongly administered by spinal injection.

- Over 6,600 adverse incidents involving medical devices were reported to the Medical Devices Agency in 1999, including 87 deaths and 345 serious injuries[10].

- Experience from the serious incident reporting system run by one of the NHS Executive's Regional Offices suggests that nationally at least 2,500 adverse events a year occur which should be serious enough to register on such systems.

- The costs to the NHS of hospital acquired infections have been estimated at nearly £1 billion a year, and around 15% of cases are regarded as preventable[11].

The Committee's task

1.16 The present Expert Committee comprised (Annex A) members from within the NHS and from some of the specialist agencies that see the results of poor quality care in the NHS, as well as consumer representation. Committee members from fields other than health care brought important experience and expertise on organisational failure, incidents and disasters from other sectors. In addition, we drew on the particular expertise of a number of external presenters and contributors. The Committee was established in February 1999 by the then Health Minister Baroness Hayman, under the Chairmanship of the Chief Medical Officer, Professor Liam Donaldson.

Terms of Reference

"To examine the extent to which the National Health Service and its constituent organisations have the capability to learn from untoward incidents and service failures so that similar occurrences are avoided in the future. To draw conclusions and make recommendations."

1.17 The Expert Committee explored fully the context and issues which underlay its terms of reference.

The Expert Committee's tasks

- Clarify the size and nature of the problem of avoidable service failure in the NHS.
- Identify the issues underlying service failure in the NHS.
- Draw on experience, research and good practice from other fields in which organisational failure and disasters have been addressed.
- Establish the best ways to identify problems, collect data and analyse them.
- Set out an approach to achieve major improvement in the way the NHS approaches this problem.

1.18 Extensive use was made of case studies and examples drawn from both health care and non-health care experience. The majority were already in the public domain, but all have been anonymised to protect individual patients and their relatives.

1.19 Experience of adverse incidents is almost entirely based on their occurrence in secondary care. It could be argued that they are more likely to happen in the organisationally complex, high technology environment of a hospital. The truth is that we simply do not know the frequency and nature of such problems occurring in primary care. The examples in this report therefore mainly concern secondary care, but its core themes and recommendations are also intended to encompass primary care. They will apply in particular to Primary Care Groups and Primary Care Trusts as they develop as organisations. In the context of the conviction of the General Practitioner Dr Harold Shipman for murdering 15 of his patients, Health Ministers also asked that our recommendations specifically addressed the situation in this sector, with particular regard to incident reporting arrangements.

CHAPTER 2

The scale and nature of the problem

In this chapter we assess what we know about the scale of the problem of adverse events in the NHS, in both human and financial terms, and illustrate briefly some of the kinds of events which occur. In fact we have relatively little reliable information to help us quantify the scale of the problem, but what there is gives at least some indication of the significance of this issue for the NHS.

Information on the scale of the problem

2.1 Table 2.1 captures, in summary form, information from a selection of the existing incident reporting and recording systems which we describe in more detail in chapter 3. It does not provide a complete or accurate picture of the scale or nature of service failures in the NHS, and indeed not all the figures cited will necessarily reflect 'adverse incidents' as opposed, for example, to unavoidable deaths. It provides some insight but must be regarded as a serious underestimate of the size of the problem. Specifically, there are no incident reporting systems which properly take account of adverse events in primary care.

2.2 Some of these statistics provide a more reliable and complete picture than others. For example coverage of statistics on suicides and homicides by mentally ill people is virtually 100%, whereas the figures from Regional incident reporting systems are unlikely to reflect anything approaching true frequency.

2.3 In the past, very little research has been undertaken to assess comprehensively the proportion of episodes of health care that result in adverse events. However, relatively recently major studies from the United States of America and Australia have yielded important data. If these are extrapolated to the NHS in England, even allowing for differences in health care systems, the estimated number of patients involved is worryingly high (Table 2.2).

Table 2.1 Information from NHS incident reporting and recording systems

Source	Event	Estimated annual number
Confidential Inquiry – Suicides and homicides	Suicides by people in recent contact with mental health services in the 12 months prior to the event	1150*
	Homicides by people in contact with mental health services in the 12 months prior to the event	40*
Confidential Enquiry - Maternal deaths	Deaths of women during pregnancy or within one year of giving birth	125#
Confidential Enquiry - Peri-operative deaths	Deaths within 30 days of surgery	20,000
Confidential Enquiry - Stillbirths and deaths in infancy	Stillbirths and infant deaths	7,800#
Complaints data	Written complaints about aspects of clinical treatment in hospitals	27,949*
	Written complaints about all aspects of treatment in primary care	38,857*
NHS Litigation Authority claims data	Clinical negligence claims settled by the Authority above local excess levels	810#
Regional Serious Untoward Incident Reporting Systems	Serious Untoward Incidents (as variously defined)	2,500 +
Medical Devices Agency medical devices	Adverse incidents involving (Including 87 deaths and 345 serious injuries)	6,610
Medicines Control Agency	Reported Adverse Drug Reactions (ADRs)	18,196* (9,819 serious)

* Most recent year for which information is available.

Average of several years

+ Extrapolated from the best-developed Regional system

Table 2.2 United States and Australian research into adverse events in hospitals

	Harvard Medical Practice Study, 1991	Quality in Australian Health Care Study, 1995
Proportion of inpatient episodes leading to harmful adverse events	3.7%	16.6% (half preventable)
Proportion of inpatient episodes resulting in permanent disability or death in which harm was also caused*	0.7%	3%
Broad extrapolation of findings to the NHS based on 8.5 million inpatient episodes a year+	314,000 potential adverse events	1,414,000 potential adverse events
	60,000 potential instances of permanent disability or death in cases where adverse events occurred*	255,000 potential instances of permanent disability or death in cases where adverse events occurred*

* It is important to emphasise that adverse events will not always be a causal or contributory factor in these cases. Many of the patients involved will have been terminally ill, and adverse events may not have played a part in causing their disability or death.

+ Extrapolated by the expert group for the purposes of the present report, not in association with the original studies.

Source: Brennan et. al.1991[12], Leape et. al. 1991[13], Wilson et. al. 1995[14]

2.4   These 'ballpark' extrapolations to the NHS in England seem to be supported by the results of a recent small-scale pilot study of hospital inpatients in London (Table 2.3).

2.5   Whilst the primary concern must of course be the human cost of service failures, there is also some information available which can help to quantify some of the financial costs of adverse events. Paid litigation claims are one example: they cost the NHS around £400 million in 1998/99, in addition to an estimated potential liability of £2.4 billion for existing and expected claims. The results of the UK pilot study on adverse events suggest that nationally the costs to the NHS of extended hospital stays as a result of adverse events could

Table 2.3 Results of a United Kingdom pilot study of adverse events in hospitalised patients

Proportion of inpatient episodes leading to harmful adverse events	10% (around half preventable)
Direct cost of additional days in hospital as a consequence of adverse events	£250,000 for 1,011 admissions
Broad extrapolation to the NHS in England based on 8.5 million inpatient episodes a year	850,000 admissions lead to adverse events
	Up to £2 billion direct cost of additional bed-days

Source: Vincent[15]

be as high as a further £2 billion a year – five times the costs of clinical negligence litigation.

Case studies

2.6 Throughout the report we draw attention to particular problems through the use of case studies which serve to illustrate the nature of the issues underlying adverse events in the NHS. In the rest of this chapter we provide examples of the kinds of adverse events which can occur and their potential consequences.

Incidents involving incorrect medication dosage

- A hospital patient collapsed after a nurse gave her antibiotic tablets crushed in water via an intravenous drip. Only special fluids can be given via an intravenous drip. Similarly, antibiotics and other drugs can only be given in specially-prepared solutions and not through the impromptu crushing of tablets. The patient was rushed to intensive care and subsequently recovered.

Source: NHS Executive

- In a three-week period two young children received double the proper dose of medication in a hospital X-ray department, prior to having a scan. In both cases their weight had been recorded in pounds, rather than kilograms. Fortunately the children suffered no ill-effects.

Source: NHS Executive

- A premature baby girl died after being given an excessive dose of morphine – 15mg instead of 0.15mg – due to miscalculation of the dosage. The dose was calculated by the Senior House Officer, checked by a nurse and administered by the Senior Registrar.

Source: NHS Executive

Incidents involving the use of technical procedures

- A number of women became pregnant following failure of earlier sterilisations which had been carried out by laparoscope (keyhole surgery). The surgeon had attached the sterilisation clips to the wrong part of the Fallopian tube.

Source: NHS Executive

- A patient had a Hickman line (plastic tube) in one of his veins to allow drugs to be administered over a long period of time. When it came for the line to be removed it was accidentally cut through and broke loose into his venous system, placing him at serious risk. He had it removed and recovered.

Source: NHS Executive

Incidents involving failures in communication

- A man admitted to hospital for an arthroscopy (an exploratory operation) on his knees had a previous history of thrombosis (blood clots). This was noted by a nurse on his admission form, but was not entered on the operation form which had a section for risk factors and known allergies. The operation was carried out and the patient was discharged from hospital the same day. Given his history of thrombosis the patient should have been given anticoagulant drugs following his operation, but because his history had not been properly recorded none were given. Two days later he was admitted to the intensive care unit of another hospital with a blood clot in his lungs.

Source: Medical Protection Society Casebook No. 13, Summer 1999

- A patient with leukaemia was about to receive a transfusion of blood platelets. The experienced senior nurse on duty in the ward noticed that there were small clumps visible in the platelet pack, and had questioned whether the transfusion should proceed. She was advised that these were probably small platelet aggregates which would be removed by a filter in the equipment. Following transfusion, the patient developed severe septicaemia and subsequently died. The platelet pack was found to be contaminated with E.-coli, a bacterium that can sometimes be present in platelets through contamination from the donor's skin. It was found on inquiry that although non-harmful platelet aggregates used to be a common feature, new processing methods had eliminated this, so that an abnormal appearance in the platelet pack should not have been accepted as of no significance. Steps were taken nationally to communicate this change to all relevant staff.

Source: NHS Executive

2.7 A graphic example of the way in which specific serious errors can be repeated a number of times over a period of years is provided by an analysis of incidents involving erroneous administration of a certain category of anti-cancer drug.

History repeating itself: Errors in spinal injections proving catastrophic

- Since 1985 at least 13 cases have occurred of people (usually children) being killed or paralysed due to the maladministration of drugs by spinal injection. The circumstances have been very similar.

Source: Review of published medical research.

2.8 Intrathecal (spinal) maladministration of drugs which should instead have been administered by the intravenous route is a rare, but always very serious, medical accident. Since 1985, 13 such accidents have been reported in medical literature or to the Committee on Safety of Medicines, but it is not known whether there are more than this because no comprehensive central record is kept of such adverse events.

2.9 Of the 13 documented maladministration accidents, 12 involved injection into the spine of an anti-cancer (cytotoxic) drug, specifically one group of drugs called vinca alkaloids (vinblastine, vincristine, and vindesine). Ten of these accidents are known to have been fatal; the final outcome is unknown in the remaining two. The two published case reports that follow are typical of this kind of incident.

Case 1

"A 10 year old boy with acute lymphoblastic leukaemia was accidentally given vindesine 4.5 mg intrathecally. After two hours he became drowsy with diplopia, third nerve palsy, and leg weakness. Folinic acid and dexamethasone were given and he made a transient recovery; 24 hours later the symptoms recurred and he died on the third day from progressive ascending paralysis. Necropsy showed leukaemic infiltration of the parietal lobes and arachnoiditis of the lumbrosacral cord and twelfth nerve nucleus – similar to the changes induced by intrathecal vincristine."
Source: Robbins et al 1985[16]

Case 2

"A patient was prescribed methotrexate 10 mg intrathecally and vincristine 2 mg intravenously as part of their chemotherapy course. The drugs were prepared ready for administration by the pharmacy department. Both syringes were sent to the ward in the same clear plastic bag. The syringes were labelled with the patient's name, the drug name, and the dose. The senior house officer gave both drugs via the intrathecal route instead of administering the vincristine intravenously as prescribed. The patient subsequently died. The doctor, who admitted at the inquest to not reading the syringe labels, was assisted by a student nurse. The doctor had not checked the syringe labels against the prescription nor verified the administration details with the nurse."
Source: Cousins and Upton 1994[17]

2.10 The vinca alkaloids are not a recent clinical development; first isolated from the periwinkle plant (Vinca rosea) in the 1950s, they were introduced into cancer chemotherapy in the 1960s. Since then, they have been widely used to treat the acute leukaemias, lymphomas, and some solid tumours. Used properly, these drugs can be very effective in the treatment of some leukaemias. However, they have long been recognised as strongly neurotoxic and can kill if incorrectly administered. They can be given safely only by the intravenous route, and should never be injected into the spine.

2.11 Product data sheets (summaries of product characteristics), package inserts, vial and pack labels, and the British National Formulary all carry prominent warnings of this hazard. For example, the data sheet for Oncovin (vincristine) carries prominent boxed warnings in three separate places, and repeats the message in the text. The pack contains an auxiliary warning sticker to be placed on syringes containing the drug, and pre-prepared syringes containing the product must be packaged in an overwrap warning label:

"**Do not remove covering until the moment of injection.**
Fatal if given intrathecally. For intravenous use only"

2.12 Despite the long-recognised neurotoxicity of vinca alkaloids, and the precautionary measures described above, disasters involving these drugs continue to occur. A case in London in 1997 led to manslaughter charges against the doctors concerned (eventually dropped by the Crown) and received widespread media attention[18,19] yet a further fatal case was reported to the Committee on Safety of Medicines the following year.

2.13 The circumstances in which vinca alkaloids are sometimes used are an important contributory factor in these accidents. In virtually all of the documented cases, the patient had been prescribed **intrathecal** methotrexate combined with **intravenous** vinca alkaloid. The two injections are then confused, or both are given by the intrathecal route. The consequences are entirely predictable. The patient may be in remission from their cancer at the time of the accident, which makes the event particularly tragic for the individual and their family. The staff concerned may face criminal proceedings, in addition to NHS and professional disciplinary processes.

2.14 The circumstances in which these incidents occur are well known. They should be entirely avoidable, but have not been eliminated. This example is taken further in section 3.13 of the next chapter to illustrate some of the underlying causal factors.

The impact of adverse events on individuals

2.15 Adverse events involve a huge personal cost to the people involved, both patients and staff. Many patients suffer increased pain, disability and psychological trauma. On occasions, when the incident is insensitively handled, patients and their families may be further traumatised when their experience is ignored, or where explanations or apologies are not forthcoming. The psycho-logical impact of the event may be further compounded by a protracted, adversarial legal process. Staff may experience shame, guilt and depression after a serious adverse event, which may again be exacerbated by follow-up action.[20,21]

2.16 The effect of adverse events on patients, their families and staff is not sufficiently appreciated and more attention should be given to ways of minimising the impact of adverse events on all those involved. These issues, while of great importance, cannot be fully addressed within this report and may require separate attention, though we made some limited comment in the context of our discussion on litigation in chapter 4.

Chapter 2 – Conclusions

- Information on the frequency and nature of adverse events in the NHS is patchy and can do no more than give an impression of the problem. Information from primary care is particularly lacking;

- International research (including a recent UK pilot study) has thrown light on the potential scale of the problems, and suggests that these may be around 850,000 adverse events each year in the NHS (range 300,000 to 1.4 million);

- The financial costs of adverse events to the NHS are difficult to estimate but undoubtedly major – probably in excess of £2 billion a year;

- There is evidence of a range of different kinds of failure, and of the recurrence of identical incidents or incidents with similar root causes;

- Case studies highlight the consequences of weaknesses in the ability of the NHS as a system to learn from serious adverse events;

- There is a need for further work focusing specifically on how the impact of adverse events on patients, their families and staff can be minimised.

CHAPTER 3

Learning from failure: evidence and experience

In this chapter we draw upon the research evidence available concerning adverse events not just in health care but across all sectors. Extensive study in non-health care fields has shown that, within most unintentional failures, there is usually no single explanatory cause for the event. Rather there is a complex interaction between a varied set of elements, including human behaviour, technological aspects of the system, socio-cultural factors and a range of organisational and procedural weaknesses. Systematic study of these issues in the health care field is sparse, but the available evidence suggests a similarly complex pattern of cause and effect relationships. Learning from adverse events is also a complex phenomenon. Yet research suggests that it is possible to identify some of the barriers that prevent organisations from learning effectively from adverse events, and to put in place measures to help overcome them.

3.1 Every year around the world major catastrophes and disasters lead to loss of life and serious injury. The text below is a reminder of some of those that have occurred in Britain. Each gave rise to huge public concern and was the subject of a formal investigation or public inquiry.

Non-health care disasters resulting in death

- Hillsborough and Bradford football ground tragedies
- Sinking of the *Marchioness* pleasure boat on the river Thames
- Manchester and Kegworth air crashes
- Southall rail crash
- Capsizing of the Zeebrugge cross-channel ferry *Herald of Free Enterprise*

3.2 Each of these catastrophes was typified by the complex set of interactions that occurred between factors which precipitated the event. In no case was there any single factor which could be deemed to have resulted in the failures, but rather an interaction between local conditions, human behaviours, social factors and organisational weaknesses. But what do we know about the factors that influence levels of hazard, the probability of failure and the ability of organisations to learn lessons when things go wrong?

3.3   Experience has been built up over many years in understanding the reasons for accidents, disasters and system failures in a number of fields. Academics have researched and written widely on the subjects of human error, risk, crisis and disaster management, as well as reliability engineering and safety management. Particular industries – for example aviation and nuclear power generation – have been conspicuous in implementing improvements based on systematic learning from accidents and incidents. Other experts have commented on the conduct of inquiries into disasters and identified the factors that appear to determine whether their findings will be implemented.

3.4   A detailed review of the research literature is beyond the scope of this report, though our references form a selected bibliography. In this chapter we highlight some of the main themes that emerge from both academic research and practical experience of preventing, analysing and managing failure of all kinds. We look first at the underlying causes of failure, and then at the factors influencing learning.

3.5   There is relatively little information to draw upon which deals specifically with the health field, though we do provide some examples. Much of the work that exists is based upon experience in the USA which bring with it a different socio-cultural and economic context in which the work is grounded. There is currently a great deal of interest in the health care sphere, following a number of well publicised serious incidents, so it is likely that research in this area will grow quickly.

Understanding the causes of failure

Human Error

"Human error should be seen as a consequence, not a cause, of failure"

3.6   There are two ways of viewing human error: the *person-centred approach* and the *system approach*. The former is still the most dominant tradition within the academic literature on failure, largely because it is more suited to the agenda of management. This approach focuses on the psychological precursors of error, such as inattention, forgetfulness and carelessness. Its associated counter-measures are aimed at individuals rather than situations and these invariably fall within the "control" paradigm of management. Such controls include disciplinary measures, writing more procedures to guide individual behaviour, or blaming, naming and shaming. Aside from treating errors as moral issues, it isolates unsafe acts from their context, thus making it very hard to uncover and eliminate recurrent error traps within the system. Though attractive from a managerial and legal perspective, as the predominant approach it is ill-suited to the healthcare domain – or to any other sphere which has high-technology elements. It is important to emphasise that this does not mean that individuals should never be held accountable for their actions.

3.7   The system approach, in contrast, takes a holistic stance on the issues of failure. It recognises that many of the problems facing organisations are complex, ill-defined and result from the interaction of a number of factors. This approach starts from the premise that humans are fallible and that errors are inevitable, even in the best run organisations (a notion captured recently in the title of the US Institute of Medicine report "To Err is Human")[22]. Errors are seen as being shaped and provoked by 'upstream' systemic factors, which include the organisation's strategy, its culture and the approach of management towards risk and uncertainty. The associated counter-measures are based on the assumption that while we cannot change the human condition we can change the conditions under which people work so as to make them less error-provoking. When an adverse event occurs, the important issue is not who made the error but how and why did the defences fail and what factors helped to create the conditions in which the errors occurred. The system approach recognises the importance of resilience within organisations and also recognises the process of learning as enhancing such resilience[23, 24, 25]. During the course of its work, the Committee was repeatedly struck by the importance of the system approach, and we return to it later in the report.

3.8   Human error is commonly blamed for failures because it is often the most readily identifiable factor operating in the period just prior to an adverse event. Yet two important facts about human error are often overlooked. First, the best people can make the worst mistakes. Second, far from being random, errors fall into recurrent patterns. The same set of circumstances can provoke similar mistakes, regardless of the people involved. Any attempt at risk management that focuses primarily upon the supposed mental processes underlying error (forgetfulness, inattention, carelessness, negligence, and the like) and does not seek out and remove these situational 'error traps' is sure to fail. The local human errors are the last and probably the least manageable part of the causal sequence leading up to some adverse event.

> "Human actions are a key element in many serious incidents but they are only part of the explanation for why disaster strikes"

3.9   All organisations operating in hazardous circumstances tend to develop barriers, defences and safeguards that become interposed between the source of the hazard and the potential victims or the losses that would occur should that risk become realised. These defences may be either 'hard' (physical containments, automation and engineered safety features) or 'soft' (the procedures, protocols, administrative controls and people at the 'sharp end'). The human elements of a system can weaken or create gaps in these defences in two ways: by *active failures* and *latent conditions* [26].

● **Active failures** are the 'unsafe acts' committed by those at the sharp end.

These can be slips, lapses, mistakes or procedural violations. They have an immediate and usually short-lived impact on the defensive layers. They also tend to occupy the spotlight in any subsequent investigation.

● **Latent conditions** are comparable to 'resident pathogens' in the body. By themselves, they often do no particular harm. They may lie dormant in the system for long periods before combining with local factors and active failures to penetrate or bypass the defences. Research has suggested that organisations can embed the preconditions for failure, and that this can take place over many years. Latent conditions arise from strategic decisions made by designers, builders, procedure-writers and top management. All such decisions have the potential for seeding 'pathogens' into the system, even good ones (hence the term 'latent condition' rather than 'latent failure'). For example, it is the business of senior management to allocate limited resources. But this is rarely done on an equitable basis. Some departments get more, others less – for what seem like sensible reasons at the time. For the latter, these shortfalls can translate into error-provoking conditions in the workplace – for example, time pressure, excessive fatigue, staff shortages, lack of experience and inadequate equipment. Unlike active failures, whose precise forms are hard to predict, latent conditions are always present. They can be identified and removed before they cause an adverse event. To use another analogy: errors and violations at the sharp end are like mosquitoes. Swat them one by one and they keep on coming. The long-lasting remedy is to drain the swamps in which they breed. The swamps are the ever-present latent conditions. However the process of addressing these latent conditions can strike at the heart of the organisation's culture or the dominant paradigm within management theory. Consequently, attempts to deal with such issues are often problematic as they require quite fundamental changes to the core beliefs and values of senior staff within the organisation.

> "The evidence from a large number of accident inquiries indicates that bad events are more often the result of error-prone situations and error-prone activities than they are of error-prone people"

3.11 One view of accident causation that has wide currency in the fields of aviation and nuclear power generation is called the 'Swiss cheese' model. This is illustrated in Figure 3.1. Ideally, all the defences separating hazards from potential losses should be intact; but, in reality, they are more like slices of Swiss cheese – full of holes. Unlike the holes in Swiss cheese, however, the gaps in system defences are continuously opening, shutting and shifting position. They are created, as discussed above, by active failures and latent conditions. Serious danger arises when a set of holes lines up to allow a brief window of accident opportunity. In hi-tech, well-defended systems (e.g. modern airliners and nuclear power plants), with many layers of barriers and safeguards, such accident opportunities are rare, but they can have devastating consequences. In many fields of clinical practice, however, there can be relatively few protective 'slices' intervening between danger and harm. In surgery, for example, very little lies between the scalpel and some untargeted nerve or blood vessel other than the skill and training of the surgeon. In health care, the human elements of the system are often the last and most important defences.

> "In health care, the human elements of the system are often the last and most important defences"

The "Swiss cheese" model of accident causation

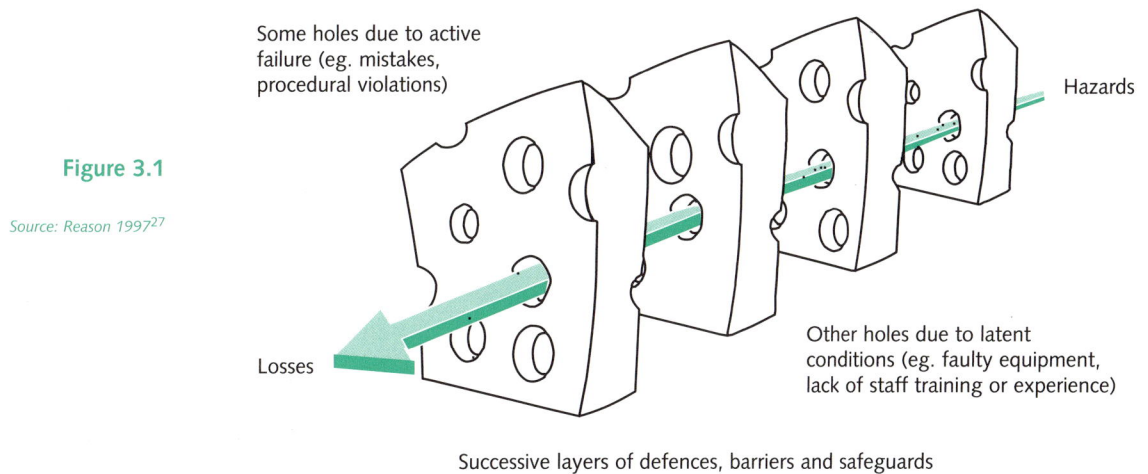

Figure 3.1

Source: Reason 1997[27]

Some holes due to active failure (eg. mistakes, procedural violations)

Hazards

Losses

Other holes due to latent conditions (eg. faulty equipment, lack of staff training or experience)

Successive layers of defences, barriers and safeguards

3.12 A good example of the need to put human error into perspective is provided by the 1989 Kegworth air crash.

Human error in perspective – the Kegworth air crash

In 1989, 47 people died when a British Midland Boeing 737-400 aircraft crashed onto the M1 motorway. The immediate act precipitating the crash was the shutdown by the crew of the wrong engine following an engine fire. The pilots were criticised for acting too quickly and for failing to assimilate information from their instruments. The official report made a number of recommendations concerning changes to the aircraft as well as pointing to the faults of the pilots and cabin staff. The media though used the shorthand of 'human error' to describe the event.

In fact the accident at Kegworth illustrated how system failure can occur at a number of levels. In the first instance there was a failure of the technical component itself which resulted from the fracture of the engine fan blades. The specific nature of this failure was not identified by the aircraft's warning system which failed to provide the pilots with unambiguous information concerning the nature of the event. There was also a failure in the decision making processes of the pilots which led to their incorrect diagnosis of the source of the engine failure and led them to close down the wrong engine. A series of communication failures compounded the problem. The pilots claimed that they were constantly distracted by communications from air traffic control and this impacted upon their reassessment of the decision to close down the right-hand engine. In addition, there was also a failure of the cabin staff and the passengers to communicate their observations of the smoke and flames from the left-hand engine.

Finally, there were a series of organisational and environmental factors that combined to create the climate in which the failure occurred. These included the design of the cockpit and its instrumentation, the protocols available for fault finding, the difficulties facing the pilots in reprogramming the automatic landing computer and the training given to the pilots to allow them to convert to a new type of aircraft.

Source: Smith 1999[28]

3.13 In the NHS too, adverse events are often the result of a series of errors or omissions leading up to the critical event itself. This is powerfully illustrated by the sequence of events leading to the death in 1997 of a young boy from maladministration of an anti-cancer drug – an issue we summarised in chapter 2. In this section we take the case study further by analysing the underlying events which led to the tragedy.

3.14 Researchers have identified a number of general factors that influence clinical practice, many of which can be related to incidents such as that illustrated in detail above. It is readily apparent that issues relating directly to the individual health care professional are only one small subset of the factors at work in clinical practice.

Factors that influence the delivery of health care

- Institutional context
- Organisational and management factors
- Work environment
- Team factors
- Individual (staff) factors
- Task factors
- Patient characteristics

Source: Vincent, Taylor-Adams and Stanhope 1998[29]

3.15 This is not to say that individuals can be absolved of their responsibilities, nor that disciplinary action is never appropriate – for example in cases involving malicious acts or gross negligence. Rather the system approach suggests that we should not automatically assume or seek out some serious, blameworthy individual failing as the principal cause of an adverse event. A focus solely on the failings of individual health care staff will miss important causes of adverse events and hamper effective learning.

The system approach to error management

3.16 Research specifically focused on health care systems suggests that as many as

An organisational accident chronology in health care: Death of a patient from maladministration of an anti-cancer drug

Sequence of events	Failures
A child was a patient in a district general hospital (DGH) and due to receive chemotherapy under general anaesthetic at a specialist centre. He should have been fasted for 6 hours before the anaesthetic, but was allowed to eat and drink before leaving the DGH.	*Fasting error. Communications problem between DGH and specialist centre.*
No beds were available for the patient on the oncology ward, so he was admitted to a mixed-specialty "outlier" ward.	*Lack of organisational resources. (i.e. beds for specialised treatments)* <hr> *Patient placed in an environment lacking oncology expertise.*
The patient's notes were lost and not available to ward staff on admission.	*Loss of patient information.*
The patient was due to receive intravenous vincristine, to be administered by a specialist oncology nurse on the ward, and intrathecal (spinal) methotrexate, to be administered in the operating theatre by an oncology Specialist Registrar. No oncology nurse specialist was available on the ward.	*Communication failure between oncology department and outlier ward.* <hr> *Absence of policy and resources to deal with the demands placed on the system by outlier wards, including shortage of specialist staff.*
Vincristine and methotrexate were transported together to the ward by a housekeeper instead of being kept separate at all times.	*Drug delivery error due to non-compliance with hospital policy, which was that the drugs must be kept separate at all times.* <hr> *Communication error. Outlier wards were not aware of this policy.*
The housekeeper who took the drugs to the ward informed staff that both drugs were to go to theatre with the patient.	*Communication error. Incorrect information communicated.* <hr> *Poor delivery practice. Allowing drugs to be delivered to outlier wards by inexperienced staff.*
The patient was consented only for intrathecal methotrexate and not for intravenous vincristine.	*Poor consenting practice. Junior doctor allowed to take consent.* <hr> *Consenting error.*
A junior doctor abbreviated the route of administration to IV and IT, instead of using the full term in capital letters.	*Poor prescribing practice.*
When the fasting error was discovered, the chemotherapy procedure was postponed from the morning to the afternoon list. The doctor who had been due to administer the intrathecal drug had booked the afternoon off and assumed that another doctor in charge of the wards that day would take over. No formal face-to-face handover was carried out between the two doctors.	*Communication failure. Poor handover of task responsibilities.* <hr> *Inappropriate task delegation.*

[continues on next page]

Sequence of events	Failures
The patient arrived in the anaesthetic room and the oncology Senior Registrar was called to administer the chemotherapy. However the doctor was unable to leave his ward and assured the anaesthetist that he should go ahead as this was a straight-forward procedure. The oncology Senior Registrar was not aware that both drugs had been delivered to theatre. The anaesthetist had the expertise to administer drugs intrathecally but had never administered chemotherapy. He injected the methotrexate intravenously and the vincristine into the patient's spine. Intrathecal injection of vincristine is almost invariably fatal, and the patient died 5 days later.	*Inadequate protocols regulating the administration of high toxicity drugs.*
	Goal conflict between ward and theatre duties. Poor practice of expecting the doctor to be in two places at the same time.
	Situational awareness error.
	Inappropriate task delegation and lack of training. Poor practice to allow chemotherapy drugs to be administered by someone with no oncology experience.
	Drug administration error.

"Research specifically focused on health care systems suggests that as many as 70% of adverse incidents are preventable"

70% of adverse incidents are preventable. However, although errors can be minimised they will never be completely eliminated – particularly where high volumes of activity occur. It has been estimated, for example, that a 600 bed teaching hospital with 99.9% error free drug ordering, dispensing and administration will experience 4,000 drug errors a year[30]. So measures also need to be taken to limit the adverse consequences of those errors that still occur. This involves designing or modifying systems so that they are better able to tolerate inevitable human errors and contain their damaging consequences.

3.17 Whilst those committed to the person approach tend to allocate the bulk of their resources to trying to make individuals less fallible, the system approach aims for a comprehensive programme directed simultaneously at people, teams, tasks, workplaces and institutions. There is no single solution which can be applied in every circumstance.

3.18 Since serious adverse events rarely have a single, isolated cause, attempts to prevent or mitigate adverse events need to address not just single event chains, but systems as a whole. While details of some future failure can hardly ever be predicted, defences can be installed that will limit their bad effects. Well-designed systems can minimise the harmful effects of errors by anticipating their occurrence and detecting them at an early stage. A simple example is the word processing package. Its designers understood that people can exit files without saving them. So they built in reminders and 'forcing functions' to make this more difficult. Similar principles can be applied to eliminating error traps in hazardous systems, and indeed to the application of design solutions. One example of the latter in health care is the development of automatically retracting syringes, which expose the needle only at the moment of injection, as an aid to the prevention of needle-stick injuries.

High-technology, high-risk procedures

3.19 High-technology, high-risk procedures have been little researched for their relevance to adverse events. However recent research suggests that particular factors can be at work in this field, and that it warrants consideration as a particularly important area of health care.

3.20 High-technology areas such as intensive care units, emergency rooms, operating theatres and high-risk medicine such as oncology, transplantation, neurosurgery, cardiac surgery and gene therapy share many similarities with other complex socio-technical systems in which people and complex technologies interact. It is logical to conclude that theories of organisation or system accidents, such as those we have discussed in this chapter, are applicable to adverse events occurring in these areas. Fatal actions in the operating theatre or in the ward are often the result of an accumulation of multiple minor and major failures, many of which may have their origins away from the immediate environment of care.

3.21 There is, however, a major difference between high-risk medicine and complex socio-technical systems such as the aviation industry. Technical advances in the latter have been such that major technical failures are rare compared to human failures. In high-risk medicine, failures may be attributable to poor patient risk (for example if a patient is in poor general health), inherent risk in some difficult treatments and/or poor performance of care providers.

"Even in cases of major human failures, appropriate compensating behaviour can prevent adverse events"

3.22 Recent research into these interactions has highlighted the role of human failures over and above the risks ascribable to particular conditions and to particular high-risk treatments. It also showed that even in cases of major human failures, appropriate compensating behaviour can prevent adverse events.[31]

3.23 The same study demonstrated that very little is done to eradicate the many small failures sometimes hardly noticed by the clinicians providing care. They were shown to have a multiplicative effect so that they became a significant risk factor. Dealing with these minor failures is one of the most challenging tasks of health care organisations. They are so subtle that most of them are not reported even in the most open incident reporting system. The employment of human factors experts as outside observers for research purposes has been extremely useful in detecting these minor failures, but whether such techniques are appropriate or feasible for more general application as a training and quality improvement tool is more questionable.

3.24 Other research has shown that for one high-risk procedure, coronary artery surgery, the rate of post-operative complications did not correlate strongly with post-operative death rates. There was however a correlation between death rates and success in rectifying complications when they did arise: the hospital with the highest mortality had a higher rate of failure to rescue from complication, rather than a higher rate of complication *per se*.[32]

3.25 What all this suggests is that to a great extent high-risk medicine is bound to be eventful and that serious errors and complications will never be eradicated, simply because there is a level of risk for which no system can fully compensate. Focusing on correction, recovery or rescue from these complications and failures – on error management as well as on error prevention – is an important and under-recognised way to improve safety in these areas. Many medical and surgical teams, whilst being perfectly capable of dealing safely with 'straightforward' cases, may not have the capacity to cope with serious adverse events. This is one of the most fundamental differences between success and failure.

Factors influencing learning from failure

3.26 So far in this chapter we have set out some key principles on the nature of error and failure, illustrating some of the complexities in this area and highlighting the importance of systems in understanding why things go wrong. In the next section we consider some of the factors which influence the ability of organisations to learn from failures when they do occur.

The learning loop

3.27 Organisational learning is a cyclical process, the key components of which can be described with reference to an approach which we have adapted from a model used by British Petroleum in the context of its work on knowledge management (Fig 3.2). Of necessity this model greatly over-simplifies the process it depicts – omitting for example the important dimension of feedback 'short circuits' within the process – but it serves to illustrate the fundamental steps in a learning cycle.

**Figure 3.2
The Learning Circle**

*Source: Adapted to health care from a
model developed by BP Amoco*

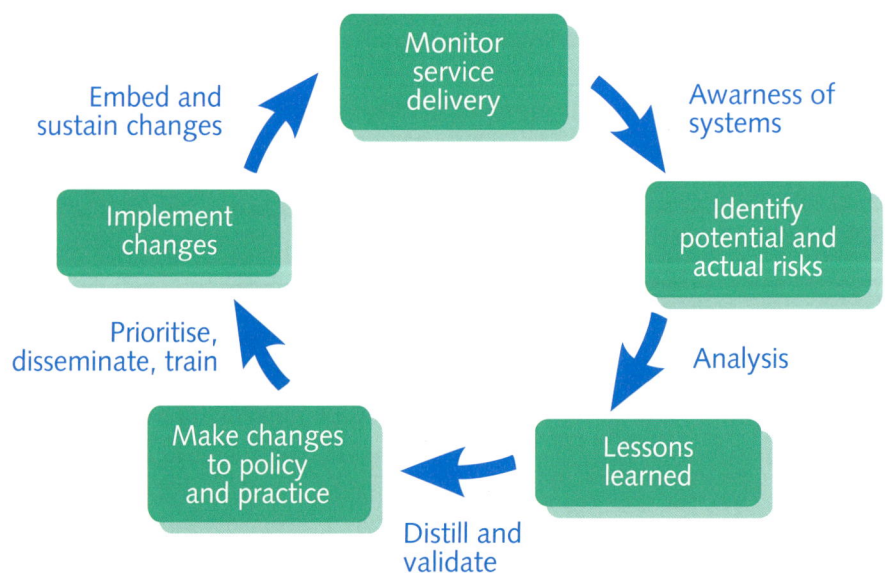

"It is difficult for
effective learning to
take place if the
initial under-
standing of what
has occurred is
seriously flawed"

3.28   The process does not differ regardless of whether learning takes place before, during or after the event. The first half of the learning cycle essentially concerns the identification of learning opportunities and the development of sound solutions. Monitoring of service delivery activity – including adverse events and the experiences of others – provides a basis for asking questions about how improvements can be brought about and errors avoided. Some commentators have suggested that a key part of this process is 'sensemaking'[33] – ensuring that individuals and organisations actually understand what the true nature of their experience is so that it provides a sound basis for learning. It is far more difficult for effective learning to take place if the initial under-standing of what has occurred is seriously flawed. In particular, it is important to consider experiences in the context of the various systems in place and the way these interact, because only in this way is it possible to come to sound conclusions about the nature of potential and actual risks faced.

3.29   Once potential and actual risks have been identified, they must be properly analysed to identify lessons for policy and practice. Lessons can be extracted from the pool of available information through analysis, but then need to be distilled – to make sure that the essence of the learning points is properly captured – and their validity tested in theory or practice. Validation is important where ideas come from experience in other sector or organisations – transferability is often possible but cannot be assumed – but it is also a key step in learning from experience within a team or an organisation. It is all too easy to reach a conclusion or draw a lesson which appears obvious, but which does not in fact stand up to testing. The initial assessment of the experience or diagnosis of the problem may be flawed, or the solution identified may not in practice address the issue effectively.

3.30   The second part of the learning process, once sound solutions have been derived, is to make sure that they are put into practice. Learning points need to be translated into practical policies and actions that can be implemented at the appropriate level. These practical changes then need to be prioritised, to provide a clear agenda for action, and disseminated to the relevant audience. Training is a vital tool in ensuring that information on change is both dissemi-nated and acted on.

3.31   Action to implement and apply improvements on the ground is an essential part of the learning process. Lessons can be 'learned' on one level, in that there is a strong awareness of what needs to change and why, but if there are barriers in place to the application of that learning in practice the active learning process will fail. However, to sustain long-term change solutions also need to be firmly embedded into the culture and routine practice of the organisation. Only if change is successfully embedded in an organisation will it survive once the "heat" is perceived to have gone out of a particular problem. If an organi-sation focuses intensively on a problem for a short period of time but forgets about it when new priorities emerge or key personnel move on, effective learning has not taken place. As we have already observed, learning is not a one-off event, it is an ongoing dynamic.

3.32 Finally, continuous monitoring of changes and improvements in practice is an essential part of ongoing learning and improvement.

3.33 All the evidence suggests that the latter stages in this learning process are critical in ensuring that organisational behaviour is actually changed as a result of the lessons drawn from adverse incidents, and that true 'learning' requires more than just the identification of valid lessons. But it is at the stages of implementation and embedding that the learning loop often seems to fracture.

3.34 The literature is replete with examples from a range of different sectors where lessons had been clearly and correctly drawn from experience, but for one reason or another these lessons had not been translated into effective organisational learning. The text below outlines four such examples – two from the NHS and two from other spheres.

Four examples of failures to close the learning loop

Bradford football ground fire
On 11 May 1985, a fire started in the main stand during a match at Bradford City's Valley Parade ground. Rubbish which had been allowed to gather beneath the wooden stand was ignited by what is believed to have been a discarded cigarette, and within a matter of minutes the stand was ablaze. 56 people lost their lives, and another 200 were injured.

As early as August 1969, the Fire Prevention Association published an article entitled "Playing safe in sporting arenas" which gave details of several fires which had taken place in football stands like the one at Bradford, and warned that "Should a fire break out, particularly if a game is in progress, a major tragedy could result."
Source: Toft 1992[34]

Taunton train fire
In the early hours of 6 July 1978 at Taunton, Devon, bed linen stored against an electric heater in a railway sleeper car caught fire and set the rest of the car ablaze. Although staff and travellers reacted with commendable speed, 12 passengers died and a further 16 were injured.

British Rail had received a warning five years previously that bed linen left on the sleeping car heater was a source of danger, following an inquiry after linen caught fire on a Glasgow-Euston train. Apparently, the lessons of the fire on the Glasgow-Euston train were not passed on because at the time of that incident all the sleeping cars on the Western Region were steam heated. Unfortunately, when the Western Region sleeping cars were converted to electric heating nobody thought to inform them of the previous incident.

Source: Toft & Reynolds 1997[35]

Suicides by mental health inpatients

For some years it has been recognised that a major means of suicide among inpatients in mental health units is hanging from curtain or shower rails. A paper drawing attention to this was first published in 1971[36]. These events can be prevented fairly simply by fitting collapsible rails which give way under the weight of a person. The 1999 report of the National Confidential Inquiry into Suicides and Homicides by People with Mental Illness concluded that hanging, and in particular hanging from non-collapsible structures such as bed and shower and curtain rails, is still the commonest method of suicide among mental health inpatients. A total of 81 mental health inpatients committed suicide on the ward by hanging in the two years to April 1998 – two thirds of all suicides which took place on the ward.

On at least one occasion a collapsible curtain rail which had given way, preventing a hanging, was incorrectly repaired. When another patient later attempted to hang himself from the same rail it failed to collapse and the patient died.

Source (suicide statistics): Safer Services 1999[37]

Death due to incorrect urinary tract irrigation

A patient with urinary tract stones underwent a procedure, under anaesthetic, in which her upper urinary tract should have been washed out with a special fluid. In fact plain water was used by mistake. The water affected the patient's bloodstream, and she suffered a fatal heart attack in the operating theatre. Despite details of the incident being circulated to all relevant hospitals, a second similar incident almost occurred within a few months in a hospital only 30 miles away. Fortunately in this case the mistake was spotted before the fluid could be administered, and no harm came to the patient. The surgeon involved pointed out that, at a distance, the bags of different irrigating fluids looked identical.

Source: NHS Executive

"It is only through active learning that the benefits of experience are actually realised"

3.35 The NHS case studies in particular are good examples of the phenomenon of 'passive' learning: valid lessons have been drawn from experience, but they have not been fully implemented. By contrast, 'active' learning involves both drawing valid conclusions and putting them into practice[38]. It is only through active learning that the benefits of experience are actually realised.

3.36 Some NHS examples of 'active learning' – where effective changes in practice do appear to have been made to prevent particular problems recurring – are provided by the 'Back to Sleep' campaign to reduce cot deaths.

The Back to Sleep Campaign – active learning in the NHS saved the lives of 3,000 babies

In the 1970s and 1980s advice given to new parents by health care professionals was that babies should be placed in their cots on their fronts. It was reasoned that if a baby regurgitated milk choking was less likely than if the baby were lying on its back.

Research from several countries, confirmed by work from Bristol published in 1990, found that babies placed on their backs had a lower incidence of 'cot death'. An expert group convened by the then Chief Medical Officer in October 1991 reviewed this and further evidence from Bristol, where the cot death rate had fallen after health care professionals started encouraging mothers to avoid prone sleeping positions in 1989.

As a result from December 1991 the Department of Health and the media ran a campaign to educate parents (the Back to Sleep campaign). Cot deaths have halved in the years since the campaign. This is an example of rapid, active learning in the NHS which led to the saving of over 3,000 babies' lives in the six years up to 1998.

Source: NHS Executive

3.37 The position of the confidential inquiries conducted in the NHS (see also paragraphs 4.40–4.43) is a half-way house between active and passive learning. It is passive because recommendations do not often lead to mandatory and immediate procedural change but rather rely on the published report to have an impact. On the other hand, because it is targeted at specific professional practitioners, some of its recommendations are taken very seriously so that a momentum for change is induced. Examples are shown at the end of chapter 4, where we discuss in more detail the NHS's capacity to implement learning from existing information sources.

Barriers to learning

"Individuals may learn from their mistakes but those around them often fail to do so"

3.38 In general, experience in the NHS and in other organisations suggests that individuals may learn from their mistakes but those around them often fail to do so. Individuals may learn because mistakes cause them emotional pain, even if they go unnoticed by others. In some cases, of course, individuals may refrain from hearing key messages as a kind of personal 'defence mechanism' – this is partly a personality feature, though people can be taught to apportion responsibility more reasonably.

Barriers to learning – an NHS example

An NHS acute psychiatric unit had been regarded by staff and managers as a troubled unit for some years. Although it had not experienced a major adverse event as such, there were acknowledged problems of an unsuitable physical environment and poor standards of care. The perception of staff working in the unit was of "a catastrophe waiting to happen". Yet it was only after a critical Mental Health Act Commission report, which described the unit as one of the worst in the country, that any action was taken.

The management team brought in to turn the unit around was ultimately successful, and two years later the unit received a national risk management award. But it took the impact of a very critical external review to galvanise the organisation into action on what had for some time been widely recognised failings. Even once the change process had begun, a number of latent barriers to learning and change – at individual, team and organisational levels – still had to be overcome.

Specific barriers identified by those brought in to turn the unit around included:

- **misdiagnosis of the real problems within the unit**. Violence and aggression had become commonplace in the unit because the standard of care had completely broken down. Rather than seeing these issues as symptoms of underlying systemic problems, the organisation initially responded to the immediate difficulties by fitting more locks, tightening security and installing a new seclusion room. These "solutions" simply exacerbated the real problem of a poor environment of care and compounded existing system failures;

- **the "closed" system within which the unit had operated**. The unit was isolated from the wider care system and therefore not open to feedback from service users and other key stakeholders. A sustained effort had to be made to lower barriers to external feedback and keep them down;

- **the inability of management to engage with the human and emotional dynamics of change**. A "macho" approach to management and care meant that staff were either emotionally "burnt out" or they were emotionally blunted and appeared uncaring. The immediate emotional needs of staff had to be addressed, and sustained through the provision of supervision and support, to enable staff to separate their own issues from the needs of their patients;

- **the failure of senior managers to acknowledge and act on concerns which had been raised repeatedly by staff**. One senior manager involved later spoke of a situation approaching "organisational denial", and staff in the unit felt frustrated and angry that the organisation had failed even to register, let alone act on, concerns which they had repeatedly raised;

- **the distracting effects of constant organisational change**. The period in which the unit had deteriorated most markedly was characterised by major changes in management structures movement among senior personnel. Senior managers "took their eye off the ball" as they became preoccupied with organisational restructuring.

Source: Presentation to the Committee on the experience of the Seymour Clinic, East Wiltshire NHS Trust. Winner of Health Service Journal Management Awards Risk Management category, 1998.

3.39 Although individuals are more likely to learn from incidents, particularly if they accept a degree of responsibility for them and/or they experience the pain of a public accident, what they learn may not always be useful. For example, it may lead to more defensive practice – perhaps keeping patients in hospital longer than is warranted. A focus on the individual makes it harder for systems to learn, to spread the impact of events or accidents beyond their immediate environment. Researchers have identified a number of 'barriers to learning' which contribute to this.

Barriers to organisational learning

- An undue focus on the immediate event rather than on the root causes of problems;
- Latching onto one superficial cause or learning point to the exclusion of more fundamental but sometimes less obvious lessons;
- Rigidity of core beliefs, values and assumptions, which may develop over time – learning is resisted if it contradicts these;
- Lack of corporate responsibility – it may be difficult, for example, to put into practice solutions which are sufficiently far-reaching;
- Ineffective communication and other information difficulties – including failure to disseminate information which is already available;
- An incremental approach to issues of risk – attempting to resolve problems through tinkering rather than tackling more fundamental change;
- Pride in individual and organisational expertise can lead to denial and to a disregard of external sources of warning – particularly if a bearer of bad news lacks legitimacy in the eyes of the individuals, teams or organisations in question;
- A tendency towards scapegoating and finding individuals to blame – rather than acknowledging and addressing deep-rooted organisational problems;
- The difficulties faced by people in "making sense" of complex events is compounded by changes among key personnel within organisations and teams;
- Human alliances lead people to "forgive" other team members their

mistakes and act defensively against ideas from outside the team;

● People are often unwilling to learn from negative events, even when it would be to their advantage;

● Contradictory imperatives – for example communication versus confidentiality;

● High stress and low job-satisfaction can have adverse effects on quality and can also engender a resistance to change;

● Inability to recognise the financial costs of failure, thus losing a powerful incentive for organisations to change.

Source: Derived from Smith and Elliot 1999[39], Firth-Cozens 2000[40], Wason 1960[41]

The importance of organisational culture

3.40 A key issue in the institutional context of adverse events is that of culture. This is important for two reasons. First, people may come and go, but an effective safety culture must persist. Second, culture is perhaps the only aspect of an organisation that is as widespread as its various defences; as such, it can exert a consistent influence on these barriers and safeguards—for good or ill. Airlines operate globally with similar equipment, training and licensing, but that the risk to passengers among different carriers varies by a factor of 42^{42}. A significant part of this variation can probably be attributed to differing 'safety cultures'.

3.41 It has been argued that safety cultures, far from being mysterious intangible entities, can be established by identifying and putting in place their key components. The process can essentially be seen as one of collective learning, or of a constant and active awareness of the potential for failure.

3.42 Experience and research studies suggest that safety is likely to be a strong feature of an **informed culture**, which has four critical sub-components[43]:

● a **reporting** culture: creating an organisational climate in which people are prepared to report their errors or near-misses. As part of this process data need to be properly analysed and fed back to staff making reports to show what action is being taken;

● a **just** culture: not a total absence of blame, but an atmosphere of trust in which people are encouraged to provide safety-related information – at the same time being clear about where the line is drawn between acceptable and unacceptable behaviours. An example is the airline safety system which we discuss later in this chapter;

● a **flexible** culture: which respects the skills and abilities of 'front line' staff and which allows control to pass to task experts on the spot; and

● a **learning** culture: the willingness and competence to draw the appropriate conclusions from its safety information system, and the will to implement major reforms where their need is indicated.

"People may come and go, but an effective safety culture must persist"

Absence of a safety culture

Non-NHS: In November 1996 an outbreak of E.-coli O157 (a serious gastro-intestinal infection sometimes carried on raw meat) occurred in Lanarkshire, Scotland, affecting around 500 people and causing at least 20 deaths. The outbreak was traced to a single butcher's shop and bakery which operated a substantial wholesale and retail trade in cooked and raw meat products. The infection had been spread from raw meat to cooked food because of inadequate food preparation, handling and hygiene standards. The business concerned had undergone considerable expansion during which insufficient attention had been paid to the maintenance of food safety.
Source: Report of the Pennington Group[44]

NHS: A young boy died in October 1998 after failing to recover from a general anaesthetic administered at a dental practice. A fatal accident inquiry concluded that the boy's death could have been prevented if a number of reasonable precautions had been in place. There was no agreement with the local hospital for rapid transfer of patients in emergencies, no heart monitor was attached when the anaesthetic was given and the anaesthetist lacked a specialist qualification. In addition, the risks of a general anaesthetic and possible treatment alternatives were not discussed with the boy's mother, the practice failed to employ a properly qualified anaesthetist's assistant and all staff lacked training in responding to medical emergencies.
Source: Fatal accident inquiry report, February 2000[45]

3.43 The potential of safety cultures to have a very positive and quantifiable impact on the performance of organisations is well-illustrated by the experience of part of the Shell oil company between 1981 and 1992.

Impact of a safety culture

In 1982, Shell Oil Tankers (UK) experienced a number of accidents in which a total of six employees lost their lives. These incidents forced the organisation to take a critical look at, for example, their safety policies, rules, regulations, operating procedures, training courses, mechanisms for learning from accidents, methods of disseminating information, methods of raising employee awareness of safety issues and their long-term strategy on safety. Thus what they actually, if unconsciously, did was to take a hard look at the safety culture of their organisation.

Following this review, the company instituted a new long-term safety management philosophy encompassing everyone who worked for the company. Components of this new approach included a visible management commitment to safety, new safety management techniques and training, more research into safety, an emphasis on learning from mistakes within the organisation and elsewhere, mechanisms for disseminating safety information, ways of motivating personnel to be safe and the fostering of a "no blame culture" so employees would feel able to admit their mistakes.

One of the key success indicators for this programme was judged to be the lost time accident frequency – a measure of the time off work lost across the organisation as a result of accidents. By 1992, the company had reduced its loss time accident frequency to one sixteenth of its 1981 level.

Source: Toft 1998[46]

Overcoming barriers to learning and creating an informed culture.

3.44 A combination of research and experience also suggests a number of ways in which some of the barriers to active learning can be overcome or minimised, helping to create informed cultures which can learn from and respond to failures.

What can we do to create an informed culture?

- **Raise awareness of the costs of not taking risk seriously.** There is a need for more routinely available data on the human and financial costs of adverse events;
- **Focus on "near misses" as well as actual incidents.** This can remove the emotion from an incident and allow learning to take place more effectively. It is also easier to keep near miss data anonymous, itself a factor in encouraging reporting;
- **Ensure that concerns can be reported without fear.** Bearers of bad news may fear that they will be ostracised or silenced: clear rules about what must be reported, and regarding reporting as good behaviour rather than as disloyalty will all help;
- **Avoid simplistic counting.** Data must be analysed and synthesised to reveal their underlying lessons;
- **Develop effectively-led teams as mechanisms for culture change.** Teams need to be firmly linked into the wider management structure to ensure that alliances within them do not hamper learning. Team-based training can also be a useful tool here.
- **Use external input to stimulate learning.** External input can help teams to think outside established parameters and challenge assumptions about the way things are done. User involvement can be of particular value in encouraging learning;

- **Ensure effective communication and feedback to front-line staff.** Teams and organisations must operate on genuinely two-way communication, not just "top down". Communication systems need to be in place to allow people to see what has changed as a result of incident or near miss reporting;
- **Give a high-profile lead on the issue.** Make it clear both nationally and locally that safety and quality are key goals;
- **Recognise staff concerns.** Try hard to emphasise the personal and service benefits of change rather than just the threats.

Source: Derived from Firth-Cozens 2000 op. cit.

Safety information systems

3.45 Detecting and accurately recording errors is a fundamental step in learning from experience. It is common-sense that we need to know what is wrong before we can take steps to put it right, but this is not always just a question of monitoring adverse outcomes. Not all unsafe systems produce bad outcomes all the time. The potential for disasters may exist, but for any number of reasons those disasters might not occur at all, or occur very rarely – what has been termed 'a dynamic non-event'.

"Near misses can be seen as a free lesson; full-blown incidents have a high human and financial cost"

3.46 If there are no bad outcomes to monitor, safety information systems need to collect, analyse and disseminate information from incidents and near misses, as well as from regular proactive checks on the system's 'vital signs'. As far back as the 1940s, research in industry demonstrated that for each accident causing serious injury, there were a far greater number of accidents which resulted in minor injuries or no injury at all – 'near misses'[47]. This phenomenon can be graphically illustrated as in figure 3.3.

3.47 Most accidents have the potential to produce serious injury but do not do so in practice – either because of some intervention or compensation or simply through good fortune. By confining analysis and learning to events which

**Figure 3.3:
The Heinrich Ratio**

After Heinrich, 1941

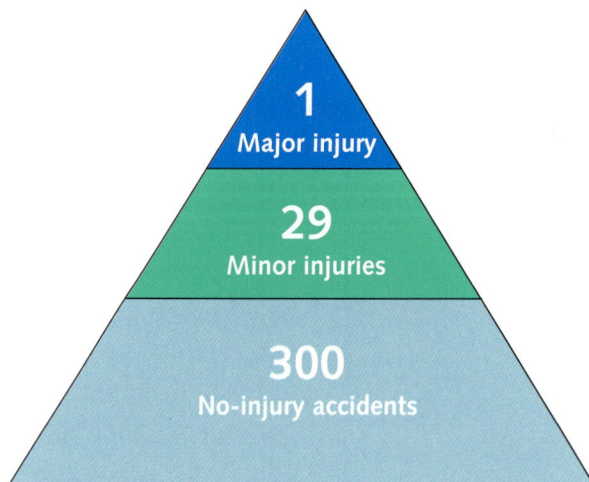

1
Major injury

29
Minor injuries

300
No-injury accidents

result in serious harm we risk skewing learning towards a very small cross-section of accidents, and may miss other important lessons for the future prevention of adverse events.

3.48 Heinrich estimated a ratio in industry of one major injury and 29 minor injuries to 300 no-injury accidents. To some extent the health of a reporting system can be judged by the proportion of minor incidents to more serious reported incidents and accidents: the greater the proportion of minor incidents reported, the better the reporting system is working.

3.49 There are practical examples of the use of 'near miss' reporting in other sectors, for example in the aviation industry which we discuss in more detail below. Some areas of activity – including the health service – may produce actual adverse outcomes on a more frequent basis, but monitoring of near misses can still highlight further issues which might not otherwise be detected.

Approaches to analysis

3.50 One of the challenges which many different sectors face is the task of both learning from and minimising the risk of so-called 'one-off' events. It is of course true to say that no specific disaster or serious incident occurs twice: each is in some way unique. However it is quite possible for an event which is on another level of analysis very similar to occur elsewhere – even in a completely different sector.

3.51 Learning from untoward events can be seen as taking place on three different levels.

Three levels of organisational learning

- individuals and organisations involved in a particular incident can each draw their own lessons from it;
- more general lessons can be drawn from an analysis of the factors surrounding an incident;
- some learning can take place simply as result of being made aware that a particular event has taken place.

Source: Toft 1992[48].

3.52 The second of these, the drawing of general lessons from individual complex, large-scale incidents (termed 'isomorphic learning' by researchers) can be a powerful tool for helping to prevent failures which, though not identical in every respect, are in some ways similar to those which have occurred previously. Researchers have suggested a number of different ways in which the task can be approached.

Types of transferable learning

Different events can create identical hazardous situations: two or more separate events may take place and manifest themselves in very different ways, but lead to the creation of what are on one level identical hazardous situations.

Different organisations can have similar experiences: different organisations operating in the same business may experience what are in essence very similar incidents.

Different kinds of organisation can have operational similarities: organisations in different lines of business may use identical or similar tools, techniques or procedures in their work, presenting similar or identical hazards.

Different parts of an organisation can have the same characteristics: where the organisation involved is very large it may have many operational sub-units which generate the same products or deliver the same services. Large companies such as Railtrack and General Motors provide examples, along with local government and – of course – the National Health Service.

Source: Toft 1992[49]

3.53 Of course there are some cautions. In particular, when looking for similarities, there is a need to guard against assuming that events which appear superficially similar are in fact similar. Just as apparently very different incidents can in fact share key common features, events which might at first look similar can in fact be very different on a more fundamental level. It is also important to guard against what has been termed 'decoy phenomenon', where attention and action is focused on a well-defined hazard while other potentially more serious problems are missed.[50]

3.54 This approach does however suggest that, given an appropriate level of analysis, organisations operating in completely different spheres can draw learning from each other's experiences of accidents or adverse events. The following brief case studies illustrate how incidents which at first seem very different can in fact have remarkable similarities.

"Organisations operating in completely different spheres can draw learning from each other's experiences of accidents or adverse events"

Misinterpretation of instruments

Non-NHS: Two airliners came close to colliding over London when an air traffic controller instructed the wrong pilot to descend. The two aircraft were circling waiting to land, but the aircraft were so close to each other on the controller's radar screen that their identity tags were difficult to read. The controller wanted the lower of the two aircraft to descend but mistakenly instructed the higher aircraft to do so. The aircraft were within approximately four hundred feet of each other when the pilot of the higher aircraft spotted the danger and climbed to safety.

Source: Toft 1999[51]

NHS: Machines called cardiotocographs (CTGs) are used to monitor and display fetal heart rate during labour. They rely on ultrasonic detection of foetal heart movement. Reports to the Medical Devices Agency revealed that several incidents occurred where, despite the fact that the monitors were showing a heart trace and gave no indication that anything was wrong, babies were delivered stillborn. It is believed that in these cases the CTG was in fact recording the maternal heartbeat rather than that of the fetus. A safety notice issued in March 1998 advised users of CTG monitors to confirm that the CTG is displaying the fetal heat rate, to use monitors in accordance with the manufacturers' instructions and not to place reliance on a single monitoring system.

Source: Safety Notice MDA SN 9813

Rogue individual behaviour within a weak management framework

Non-NHS: On 26 February 1995 Barings Bank was forced into receivership owing £840 million. The collapse was caused by a rogue trader, Nick Leeson, who had deliberately circumvented established company rules and regulations to engage in high-risk trading activity. The board of the bank had been aware that such abuse was technically possible, but did not perceive the risk as being real because they did not believe that a member of their staff would behave in this way.

Source: Contemporary media reports

NHS: During the months February to April of 1991, Beverley Allitt, a nurse on the children's ward at Grantham and Kesteven General Hospital, killed four children in her care and harmed nine others by a variety of methods. The independent inquiry into these incidents identified shortcomings in the management and organisation of the hospital, citing lax operational procedures and failure to act quickly and decisively on suspicions of foul play. It concluded that these failings contributed to the vulnerability of the unit to this kind of rogue individual behaviour.

Source: The Allitt Inquiry, 1994[52]

Staff acting beyond their competence in critical situations

Non-NHS: A young student tenant died from carbon monoxide poisoning following the installation of an inappropriate type of boiler in the bathroom of her flat. The actual installation of the boiler was also carried out to an unacceptable standard. During the subsequent trial the court was told that the gas fitter was not competent to install the boiler nor was he registered with the Council for Registered Gas Installers (CORGI) as required by law.

Source: Toft 1999[53]

NHS: An unaccredited perfusionist (technician) was allowed to work unsupervised following major heart surgery on a baby in 1998. A blood filter was inserted incorrectly into the heart bypass machine which he was supervising, and the machine failed. Although the Coroner concluded that the baby was already fatally ill before the machine failed, under other circumstances such a failure would almost certainly have been fatal.

Source: NHS Executive

Using equipment for a purpose which was not intended

Non-NHS: An engineer checking a high-pressure water pump indicator light on a control panel at a nuclear power plant in Japan left an aluminium rod, which he should not have been using, inside the computer he was working on. The rod caused a short-circuit which created a false signal leading the reactor's computer to conclude that one of the three pumps used for circulating water in the reactor was working when it was not. As a result the computer turned off the other two pumps. This action caused a large rise in temperature to occur forcing the automatic emergency core cooling system into operation and a rapid shutdown of the reactor.

Source: Toft 1999[54]

NHS: In 1996, four babies contracted the same type of serious infection at a neonatal unit in the West Midlands. Two died and one had to have part of a limb amputated. The organism causing the infection was traced to wooden tongue depressors which were being used as splints to immobilise limbs for the insertion of intravenous lines. This was ad hoc adaptation of a piece of equipment with disastrous consequences. The Medical Devices Agency (MDA) advised hospitals to stop using wooden tongue depressors as limb splints, to use proper splinting materials and to ensure that nursing procedures required skin under splints to be checked regularly.

Source: Hazard Notice MDA HN 9604

Warnings ignored

Non-NHS: 144 people, including 116 children, died at Aberfan, South Wales in October 1966 when a large amount of coal mining waste slipped down a hillside and engulfed part of the village. Over the years there had been many warnings from the local population about the dangers the tip posed, especially after a number of previous slips. However, no remedial action was taken by those responsible to rectify the situation.

Source: Toft & Reynolds 1997[55]

NHS: In September 1994, a man suffering from paranoid schizophrenia ran over and killed a stranger. He was charged with murder but found unfit to plead and was detained in a high security hospital. The man had a history of severe mental illness stretching back over 10 years and had been admitted to hospital on a number of occasions. His condition deteriorated while his social worker was on leave, but despite the fact that a neighbour and drop-in centre workers raised concerns with social services nothing was done until the social worker returned. The social worker visited once more a few days later after a neighbour again raised concerns, but the subsequent inquiry commented that his "possible need for hospital treatment was not met". Shortly afterwards he ran over and killed a woman in a car park.

Source: Main et. al. 1996[56]

"With hindsight it is easy to see a disaster waiting to happen. We need to develop the capability to achieve the much more difficult – to spot one coming"

Dangerous omissions

Non-NHS: An aircraft of the Royal Flight was forced to make an emergency landing when the aircrew noticed that all four of the aircraft's engines were experiencing a significant drop in oil pressure. Before landing the pilot had to shut down two of the engines and a third as they taxied on the runway. Upon investigation, the cause of the problem was found to be that none of the engine oil seals had been replaced during routine maintenance and so when the engines were running they were all losing oil.

Source: Toft 1999[57]

NHS: Two patients died in separate incidents when partially-used containers of intravenous fluid were reconnected to administration sets. Both patients suffered fatal air embolisms (air bubbles in the bloodstream). A subsequent MDA safety notice emphasised that partially-used intravenous fluid containers should always be discarded because re-use increases the risk of both air embolism and infection.

Source: Hazard Notice MDA HN 9702

Systems for learning from experience – the example of the aviation industry

3.55 Some industries have invested significant resources in developing systems to gather and analyse information on service failures and to ensure that lessons are systematically implemented. The best examples tend to occur in sectors where real-life experience has shown that the potential consequences of failures are high in human, environmental or financial terms – for example the oil, nuclear and airline industries. A comprehensive review of these systems is beyond the scope of this report, but some valuable insights can be gleaned from a brief review of what is probably the best-developed system, that operated by the airline industry.

3.56 The Aviation Safety System operates internationally, though reporting of lower-level incidents in particular is better-developed in some countries than in others. The system has five principal components, which combine to provide a means of detecting, analysing and acting on actual incidents and "near misses" or other errors, along with proactive identification of issues which have the potential to pose a safety risk if left unchecked.

Components of the aviation safety system

- **Accident and serious incident investigations,** governed by the International Convention on International Civil Aviation (ICAO) Accident/Incident Data Reporting Programme (ADREP). ADREP includes provision for the international dissemination of investigation reports.
- **The Mandatory Occurrence Reporting Scheme (MORS),** which provides a mechanism for notifying and reporting a range of adverse occurrences regardless of whether they result in an accident. MORS feeds into a database at national level for trend analysis and feedback to the industry.
- **The Confidential Human Factors Incident Reporting Programme (CHIRP),** which is administered by an independent body and which provides sensitive follow-up and feedback on reports of human errors that have been rendered anonymous.
- **Company safety information systems,** such as British Airways' BASIS system, which record all levels of safety-related incidents. Information is shared on a peer basis within systems, and staff report with an explicit reassurance that no individual will be pursued for an honest mistake.
- **Operational monitoring systems,** which proactively monitor crew competency through regular checks and review Flight Data Recorder information from every flight. There is management/union agreement on handling of any incidents or failures detected in this way.

3.57 The focus of the system is on detecting and learning from not only accidents and serious incidents, but also lower-level incidents or near misses, some of which might have the potential to lead to a more serious occurrence. The

"In aviation the great majority of learning is extracted not from accidents themselves but from incidents which had the potential to result in accidents"

aviation safety system receives reports of around 600 incidents, 30 serious incidents and 10 accidents for every one fatal accident. Thus in aviation the great majority of learning is extracted not from accidents themselves but from incidents which had the potential to result in accidents.

3.58 Yet the aviation safety information system has not always been so well-developed. Advances over the last ten years demonstrate the potential greatly to improve organisations' incident reporting systems in a relatively short space of time if the issue is given sufficient priority.

The situation which led to the establishment of the British Airways safety information system (BASIS)

"In 1989 British Airways possessed 47 four-drawer filing cabinets full of the results of past investigations. Most of this paperwork had only historic value. An army of personnel would have been required if the files were to be comprehensively examined for trends or to produce useful analyses."

Captain Mike Holton, Senior Manager Safety Services, British Airways Plc.

3.59 From research on the characteristics of effective safety information systems, together with experience from the aviation industry, we can draw a number of conclusions about the characteristics of effective incident reporting systems.

Characteristics of effective incident reporting systems

- separation of collection and analysis from disciplinary or regulatory bodies
- collection of information on "near misses" as well as actual incidents
- rapid, useful, accessible and intelligible feedback to the reporting community
- ease of making a report
- standardised reporting systems within organisations
- a working assumption that individuals should be thanked for reporting incidents, rather than automatically blamed for what has gone wrong
- mandatory reporting
- standardised risk assessment – i.e. a common understanding of what factors are important in determining risk
- the potential for confidential or de-identified reporting

Chapter 3 – Conclusions

- Awareness of the nature, causes and incidence of failures is a vital component of prevention – ("You can't know what you don't know");

- Analysis of failures needs to look at root causes, not just proximal events; human errors cannot sensibly be considered in isolation of wider processes and systems.

- Error reduction and error management systems can help to prevent or mitigate the effects of individual failures;

- Certain categories of high-risk, high-technology medicine might be regarded as special cases. In these areas the level of endemic risk is such that serious errors or complications will never be eradicated. The evidence suggests that here a focus on compensating for and recovering from adverse events might be an important part of the approach to improving safety and outcomes;

- Organisational learning is a cyclical process, and all the right components must be in place for effective, active learning to take place. Distilling appropriate lessons from failures is not enough: there is a need to embed this learning in practice, and it is at this stage that the "learning loop" often fails;

- It is possible to identify a number of important barriers to learning which must be overcome if the lessons of adverse incidents are to be translated into changes in practice;

- Culture is a crucial component in learning effectively from failures: cultural considerations are significant in all parts of the learning loop, from initial incident identification and reporting to embedding appropriate changes in practice. Safety cultures can have a positive and quantifiable impact on the performance of organisations;

- Sound safety information systems are a precondition for systematic learning from failures. They need to take account of the fact that low-level incidents or "near misses" can provide a useful barometer of more serious risks, and can allow lessons to be learned before a major incident occurs;

- Given appropriate approaches to analysis, it is possible to identify common themes or characteristics in failures which should be of use in helping to predict and prevent future adverse events;

- The NHS is not unique: other sectors have experience of learning from failures which is of relevance to the NHS.

CHAPTER 4

Strengths and weaknesses of NHS mechanisms for learning from adverse events

In this chapter we set out recently implemented arrangements for quality improvement in the NHS. We then review the approaches that are currently taken to learning from incidents and service failures in the NHS, which have not so far been a major part of the NHS modernisation programme. Some reporting systems are in place for major incidents, but they vary in their approach and operate with differing degrees of formality. There is no standardisation or definition of what constitutes an incident or adverse event for reporting purposes. There is no national system whatsoever for gathering information on serious incidents where a catastrophe or serious incident has been averted ('near misses').

Particular strengths of the present system are the development work which has been undertaken on risk management over the last few years and the professionally-led Confidential Inquiries which aim to identify avoidable factors which lead to poor outcomes of care in certain fields. Despite this there is little doubt that the lack of a comprehensive and purpose-designed system of information gathering, the absence of a 'reporting culture' and the patchiness of mechanisms for learning are weaknesses of the NHS at present.

The context: An NHS quality framework

4.1 Assuring and improving the quality and safety of NHS clinical services is a key theme of the current Government's health service modernisation strategy. Following on from *The new NHS* White Paper, the consultation document *A First Class Service: Quality in the new NHS* set out a three-pronged approach to NHS quality improvement, comprising:

- Clear national quality standards: set by a new National Institute for Clinical Excellence (NICE) and National Service Frameworks (NSFs);

- Dependable local delivery: through systems of clinical governance in NHS organisations;

- Strong monitoring mechanisms: a new statutory Commission for Health Improvement, an NHS Performance Assessment Framework and a national survey of NHS patient and user experience.

4.2   This new national approach to quality improvement should over time have a positive impact on the development of local capacity to detect, prevent and learn from service failures. The introduction of local systems of clinical governance is particularly relevant to the development of NHS organisations' predisposition to learn from failures. The three main components of local clinical governance arrangements are:

- clear arrangements for accountability and reporting, with ultimate Board level responsibility for arrangements to assure and improve quality;

- a coherent programme of quality improvement activity; and

- risk management processes, including mechanisms for detecting and dealing with poor professional performance.

4.3   NHS organisations are due to produce their first annual clinical governance reports later this year, but as has been explicitly recognised there is considerable variation in states of readiness for the development of clinical governance and it should be seen as a medium to long-term development objective. It is also very pertinent to ask how well current mechanisms for learning from experience appear to support NHS organisations in improving the quality and safety of the care they provide.

Risk management in the NHS

4.4   Further important context is provided by the development of risk management systems in the NHS. Adverse clinical events are of course one of the many risks which NHS organisations face, and must to some extent be seen in that wider context.

4.5   There has been a concerted drive during the 1990s to develop risk assessment and risk management systems within NHS organisations. This work was initially focused on reducing litigation risks and subsequently – with the broadening of the concept of Controls Assurance – on the reduction of financial risks and ensuring probity. More recently the NHS Executive has emphasised the importance of developing holistic approaches to risk management, not least in recognition of the fact that it can be difficult to differentiate between 'clinical' and 'non-clinical' risk management. There have also been moves to encourage a broader focus on adverse events, rather than simply on litigation.

4.6   In combination, the introduction of clinical governance and the expansion of controls assurance beyond purely financial risks provide a strong impetus for the further development of comprehensive local risk assessment and risk management systems, of which sound local incident reporting mechanisms are a particularly important part.

Poorly-performing clinicians

4.7   It is important to recognise that the great majority of adverse events are not indicative of or attributable to deep-seated problems of poor performance on the part of individual clinicians. As we have already discussed, the causes of errors are manifold and complex, and can rarely be attributed solely to the actions of one individual. But there are inevitably some links between sub-standard professional performance and adverse events. In particular, in health care, action to prevent recurrence may need to be directed at an individual or a team as well as at organisational systems.

4.8   The Government published last year a consultation document setting out proposals for new ways of preventing, recognising and dealing with poor performance among doctors specifically[58]. That document emphasised the importance of exploring thoroughly apparent poor performance problems to ensure that the root causes of any problems can be accurately identified and dealt with, and it specifically recognised the likelihood that a systematic examination of some professional performance issues may well reveal deeper and more complex problems within organisations. Similarly, it is possible that systems for detecting and analysing adverse events might provide indications of emerging problems with a particular clinician. Although poor professional performance and adverse clinical events are very distinct issues, it is therefore important that systems put in place for detecting and addressing each of these problems can link with and refer to the mechanisms for tackling the other.

Current NHS mechanisms for learning from adverse events

"There are no universally accepted criteria for identifying the occurrences or outcomes of health care that should constitute a basis for recording or reporting poor quality"

4.9   There are no universally accepted criteria for identifying the occurrences or outcomes of health care that should constitute a basis for recording or reporting poor quality. Neither does the NHS have a single comprehensive system of gathering data to enable service failure to be recognised, but information is available from different sources. Some are specifically set up to monitor adverse events, whilst others are designed to gather more general health information.

Current systems that can yield information on adverse incidents

- Incident reporting systems (e.g. local risk reporting systems in NHS Trusts and other bodies, untoward incident schemes run in NHS regions, reporting of adverse reaction to medicines and medical devices).

- Data derived as a by-product of systems designed to investigate or respond to instances of poor quality care (e.g. litigation for alleged medical negligence, the NHS complaints procedure, cases referred to the Health Services Commissioner, Coroner's cases).
- Databases of on-going studies on a national basis which aim to identify poor outcomes and avoidable factors in certain specific fields of health care (in particular the confidential enquiries into peri-operative death, maternal mortality, stillbirth and infant deaths, homicides and suicides by mentally ill people).
- Periodic external studies and reviews (e.g. the national Value for Money studies conducted by the Audit Commission).
- Spontaneous reporting outside normal channels by individual members of staff (sometimes know as "whistleblowing").
- Health service and public health statistics.

4.10 In addition, the NHS makes a considerable investment in ad hoc inquiries of various kinds in its attempts to extract learning from specific incidents.

4.11 These sources of information give a very incomplete picture of the size and nature of the problem of service failure and adverse events in the NHS. Their strengths and weaknesses, as well as what can be derived from them, are considered in the next few sections.

Incident reporting systems

4.12 The concept of an untoward incident is one which has grown up within the NHS over the years. It is a loosely used term for which there is no standardised definition:

Some characteristics of untoward incidents in the NHS

- a serious event in which a patient or patients were harmed or could have been harmed;
- the event was unexpected;
- the event would be likely to give rise to serious public concern or criticism of the service involved.

"Some extant NHS guidance on untoward incident reporting dates from 1955"

4.13 Formal Department of Health guidance on untoward incident reporting was first issued in 1955. Somewhat surprisingly, this guidance is still current. Incident reporting has also been addressed in subsequent guidance and in the recommendations of major independent incident inquiries.

Guidance and recommendations on incident reporting in the NHS

". . . a brief report should be prepared by the Secretary of the Board of Governors or Hospital Management Committee as soon as possible after any occurrence of the kind in question, giving the name of any person injured, the names of all witnesses, details of the injuries and the full facts of the occurrence and of the action taken at the time . . ."

[H.M.(55)66: National Health Service – Reporting of Accidents in Hospitals. Ministry of Health, July 1955]

- a procedure should be devised and implemented, covering the action to be taken by line managers in the event of an incident involving actual or potential loss, injury or damage
- all incidents involving actual or potential injury, loss or damage should be reported immediately
- a simple reporting procedure using no more than two forms should be introduced
- a designated individual should be responsible for initiating further communication or enquiries and ensuring that appropriate action is taken."

[Risk Management in the NHS. NHS Executive 1993 (reissued 1996)]

"reports of serious untoward incidents to District and Regional Health Authorities should be made in writing and through a single channel which is known to all involved."

[Sir Cecil Clothier (Chairman), The Allitt Inquiry, HMSO February 1994]

". . . there must be a quick route to ensure that serious matters . . . are reported in writing to the Chief Executive of the hospital, and in the case of directly managed units, to the District Health Authority. All District Health Authorities and NHS Trust Boards should take steps immediately to ensure that such arrangements are in place."

[EL(94)16 Report of the independent inquiry relating to deaths and injuries on the children's ward at Grantham and Kesteven General Hospital during the period February to April 1991 ("the Allitt Inquiry") – NHS Executive, 1994]

"Now that Regional Offices are in place it is appropriate for them to be formally notified of serious untoward incidents, whether these occur in NHS Trusts or DMUs. I should therefore be grateful if you could discuss with Trust Chief Executives the best means of instituting arrangements whereby you are informed in writing of any such incidents."

[Letter to NHS Executive Regional Directors from J F Shaw, Director of Corporate Affairs, NHS Executive, 10 May 1995]

"explicit arrangements (or protocols) for the reporting of serious untoward incidents from the NHS to Regional Offices should be in place following

NHS Executive guidance issued in May 1995 in the wake of the Beverley Allitt case."

[Sir William Wells (Chairman) – Kent & Canterbury screening report – October 1997]

"Criterion 13: Incidents, including ill health, are systematically identified, recorded and reported to management in accordance with an agreed policy of positive, non-punitive reporting.
Criterion 16: All reportable incidents are communicated to the relevant external body in accordance with relevant reporting requirements."

[Controls Assurance Standard: Risk Management System (Core Standard). NHS Executive, November 1999]

4.14 The Clinical Negligence Scheme for Trusts (CNST) was established in 1995 and almost all NHS Trusts are members. It requires, as a condition of discounted premiums, the development of clinical incident reporting systems for compliance with its risk management standards. NHS Trusts must have basic systems in place across some of the organisation to attain even the most basic level of CNST standards, and have to develop a comprehensive system to reach the highest level, level 3. The requirement as part of clinical governance for the development of clear clinical risk management policies provides further impetus for the development of local reporting systems.

4.15 The evidence suggests that historically incident reporting has been rather haphazard. Today, although the great majority of NHS Trusts have some form of incident reporting system in place, there is substantial variation in the coverage and sophistication of these systems.

Status of incident reporting in NHS Trusts

- a fifth do not have reporting systems covering the whole organisation
- less than half provide specific training on risk management or incident reporting
- less than a third provide guidance to staff on what to report
- a third do not require clinicians to report unexpected operational complications or unexpected events
- rates of reporting vary widely

Source: Dineen and Walsh 1999[59]

4.16 Experience of reporting systems at Regional level is also variable. The eight Regional Offices of the NHS Executive have approached the requirement to establish incident reporting in their regions in different ways. All have put in place protocols and mechanisms of some kind, but these vary considerably in their nature and sophistication. They have tended to focus primarily on the immediate handling issues around incidents, rather than on systematic recording. The longest-established system is that which has been operated since 1995 by the NHS Executive's Northern and Yorkshire Regional Office.

Regional incident reporting – good practice

In 1995, the Northern and Yorkshire Regional Office of the NHS Executive set up a standardised untoward incident reporting system. Examples of serious incidents are given and a serious untoward incident is defined. NHS Trusts and health authorities are asked to notify the Regional Office as soon as possible after a serious untoward incident. An electronic database was established in 1997 to facilitate the reporting and review of incidents. It can be interrogated for brief summary reports and is being further refined to include categorisation of incidents by care sector. There are explicit requirements set out for reporting, for conducting inquiries, for disseminating their findings and acting on the lessons learned.

4.17   The numbers of serious incidents reported to each region are shown in Table 4.1. They must be taken as a very crude reflection of all such occurrences especially in the regions which have less developed incident reporting systems. The Northern and Yorkshire database gives an indication of which sector the incidents fall into. Although not all regions can provide this level of analysis, most have informed us that incidents in mental health services account for about half the total each year. This is likely in part to be a reflection of higher reporting levels for incidents involving mental health services – for which there

Table 4.1 Numbers of incidents reported to NHS Executive Regional Offices in England (1998)

Region	Number of Incidents
Trent	82
South Eastern	150[1]
Eastern	150–200[1]
North West	110–120[2]
Northern and Yorkshire	361
London	180[1]
West Midlands	122[3]
South and West	120[1]

1   Region's estimate of number of reported incidents per annum. Boundary changes mean that figures are not available by current RO.

2   Mental health incidents only. No formal recording procedure for other incidents

3   Number of incident briefings provided June 1997 to February 1999

are specific reporting requirements – and cannot be taken as an accurate representation of the relative numbers of actual incidents.

Current regional incident reporting systems fulfil a number of purposes:

- creating an opportunity to make an intervention to resolve or handle a problem;
- gathering information to learn from the adverse event and prevent similar occurrences in the future;
- advising Health Ministers of the existence of the problem;
- alerting government and NHS Press Officers that there is likely to be media coverage and advising on how this should be handled.

4.18 From our review of incident reporting systems we concluded there were a number of serious weaknesses:

Weaknesses in current NHS incident reporting systems

- There is no standardised, operational definition of "adverse event" which would be easily understood by all NHS staff.
- The coverage and sophistication of local incident reporting systems, and the priority afforded to them by NHS Trusts, varies widely. Incident reporting in primary care is largely ignored.
- Regional Offices of the NHS Executive are charged with establishing and maintaining systems for reporting and monitoring incidents beyond the organisations immediately concerned, but there are major differences in the approach taken in the eight parts of the country.
- The regional incident reporting systems undoubtedly miss some serious incidents and take hardly any account of less serious incidents or those which do not harm patients but might have done.
- There is no standardised approach to investigating serious incidents at any level. Most involve internal enquiries, some involve external enquiries but the way in which a decision is taken or how they are carried out is inconsistent.
- Current systems do not facilitate learning across the NHS as a whole.

4.19 To some extent this situation may reflect both the culture of devolved responsibility and competition under the internal market of the early to mid 1990s and the major structural changes which occurred at Regional level during the same period.

4.20 In addition to the local and regional incident reporting mechanisms described above, specific systems exist for the reporting of adverse reactions to drugs and errors involving medical devices.

Reporting of adverse reactions to drugs

4.21 Information is limited on the safety of medicine at the time of licensing, since clinical trials are generally carried out on relatively small numbers of subjects and in carefully defined populations. All drugs have the potential to cause adverse reactions and spontaneous reporting schemes are the only practical method of monitoring the safety of all drugs throughout their use in clinical practice. Therefore, encouraging spontaneous reporting of adverse drug reactions (ADRs) is an essential part of establishing the safety profile of a medicine in clinical use.

4.22 The Medicines Control Agency (MCA) administers a single system – the "Yellow Card" scheme- for reporting ADRs in England, Scotland and Wales. The principal purpose of spontaneous reporting is to identify previously unrecognised potential drug safety hazards. In this respect the Yellow Card Scheme has proved to be one of the most effective in the world.

The Yellow Card scheme

The Yellow Card scheme has been in operation since 1964. Reporters of suspected adverse drug reactions (ADRs) are doctors, dentists, coroners and hospital pharmacists. Reports are received directly from them and from pharmaceutical companies relating to the drugs for which they hold Marketing Authorisations. The scheme is voluntary for health professionals, whereas Marketing Authorisations holders are required to report serious ADRs to the MCA within 15 days of notification. Since 1964 more than 350,000 UK reports of suspected adverse reactions have been received. Reporting levels are quite consistent and there is good co-operation from health professionals. Facilities for electronic reporting are being introduced to improve the speed and ease of the process and help reduce under-reporting.

Marketing Authorisations are regularly updated as new information arises to ensure that prescribers and patients have sufficient information to allow the safe and effective use of medicines.

4.23 The limitations of the scheme are well recognised. In particular, there is a variable degree of under-reporting and there have been recent initiatives to try to combat this.

4.24 Spontaneous reporting data must be interpreted with care. Doctors are asked to report suspected ADRs and a report of a suspected adverse reaction does not necessarily imply a causal relationship with the drug. Nor does an ADR necessarily imply an error in the drug's prescribing or administration.

Reporting of adverse incidents involving medical devices

4.25 Adverse incidents involving medical devices are reported to the Medical Devices Agency (MDA). Information is logged on a central database, containing details of over 48,000 incidents. Incidents are assigned to a level of investigation depending on the risks involved.

4.26 Outcomes of investigations are subject to a formal review. Patterns or clusters of incidents can then be identified, subjected to further risk assessment procedures and investigated where necessary.

4.27 When an incident reveals a device-related safety problem the MDA produces a Hazard or Safety Notice for distribution.

Medical Devices Agency notices and bulletins

Hazard Notices are used in the most serious cases, when either a patient's health (or life) has been put at risk, or staff safety has been compromised, either by a device fault or an operator error. They require immediate action when received by healthcare organisations.

Safety Notices are issued when it is clear that a potential safety problem exist with a medical device. They call for action to avoid the risk, often involving alerting staff, or altering procedures either for use or maintenance of the equipment.

Device Bulletins are longer publications produced when device management changes are needed for safe and effective device use, and

Pacemaker Technical Notes are dedicated to advice relating to pacemakers and are distributed directly to pacing centres.

4.28 Each year the MDA reminds the whole of the health care sector how to report an adverse incident, through publication of a Safety Notice. The annual notice describes what an adverse incident is, what to report, how to report it and gives statistics for the previous year.

Reports to the Medical Devices Agency (1999)

- 6,610 reports of adverse incidents
- 37% manufacturing problems (design, quality control, packaging etc.)

- 27% device faults which developed during use
- 12% user error
- 24% displayed no links to the device failure

Source: MDA

Complaints

4.29 A single NHS complaints system was introduced in 1996 for hospitals, community health services and family health services. Complaints to NHS organisations are first addressed by local services, with the aim of resolving the issue (often informally) as quickly as possible. Unresolved complaints are subject to a further review which may result in consideration by an Independent Review Panel. The panel will investigate the complaint and produce a written report, which may make comments and recommendations about the circumstances of the complaint and the need for service improvements.

4.30 If complainants are not satisfied with the response from the NHS, they may refer the matter to the Health Service Commissioner. The Commissioner's jurisdiction was extended in 1996 to cover complaints about clinical judgement and family health services, to enable him to look at complaints about all aspects of NHS care. The Health Service Commissioner publishes an annual overview and more detailed six-monthly reports on complaint investigations, which may contain recommendations for changes in practice.

4.31 National complaints statistics are published annually but have historically been used more to monitor how the system is working rather than to focus on the substance of the complaints themselves.

NHS complaints (1998–99)

- 86,013 written complaints made about hospital care
- 38, 857 written complaints made about family health services
- 27,949 hospital complaints concerned "aspects of clinical treatment"
- 285 hospital and 313 family health services complaints were referred for independent review
- there is no information nationally on the number of complaints which are "upheld"

Source: Department of Health 2000[60]

4.32 Complaints reviews are one source of qualitative information about service failures and may highlight the need for particular improvements. The system as a whole does not provide a reliable picture of the number or types of service

"Information from complaints is under-exploited as a learning resource"

failures experienced in the NHS. Nor, as presently organised, does it provide any basis for learning across the NHS as a whole. It is only the small number of complaints considered by the Health Service Commissioner that enable (through his publications) issues of relevance to the NHS as a whole to be identified. There is no evidence to show the extent to which individual NHS organisations learn from complaints though this is one of the requirements of clinical governance. Overall, we believe that information from complaints is under-exploited as a learning resource, particularly at national level. The NHS Executive's evaluation of the operation of the complaints system, which is due to report early in 2001, may provide one opportunity for addressing some of these concerns.

Learning from clinical litigation

4.33 It was not within the Committee's remit to focus in any major way on the issue of clinical negligence litigation. Inevitably, though, litigation did form part of our deliberations, for a number of reasons:

- It represents a very visible manifestation of adverse outcomes of care, which are damaging to patients and their families as well as costly to the NHS;

- Many of the injuries to patients that result in litigation are judged in retrospect to have been potentially avoidable;

- Data from litigation claims represent a potentially rich source of learning from failure;

- Only a small proportion of potential negligence claims are pursued through to court. There is a tremendous amount of unutilised data, beyond high-profile court cases, which provides a further potential source for learning;

- It is a very significant part of the resource costs of adverse incidents to the NHS, with a cash outlay of around £400 million a year in addition to an estimated potential liability of £2.4 billion – for existing claims and incidents which may result in claims – spread over a number of years;

- The processes of dealing with adverse events which lead to litigation are often themselves perceived by patients as a further element of poor care. Thus there are lessons to be learned and improvements to be made to procedures for dealing with the aftermath of adverse events. For example the NHS needs to move away from a position where the automatic response to complaints and claims is often very defensive, towards one which is much more open. A common criticism, though one which is beginning to be addressed, is that the NHS is bad at admitting its mistakes and offering patients an apology. The NHS Litigation Authority has addressed this point in guidance, but change in attitudes and practice is gradual;

4.34 The possible impact of creating an effective 'learning loop' to derive benefit from clinical litigation information is illustrated by an example from the field of obstetrics and midwifery. A substantial proportion of the money paid out in clinical litigation settlements by the NHS each year arises from obstetric problems which result in the birth of babies which result in significant brain damage and permanent serious disabilities, such that they are handicapped for life. The birth of a brain-damaged baby is not always due to clinical error, but a number of consistent factors contribute to those cases which do involve negligence.

Brain damage to babies at the time of birth – key facts

- The average sum awarded is around £1.5 million, with some awards as high as £4 million;
- Claims account for 50% of the NHS litigation bill every year;
- A 10% reduction in the number of adverse events causing brain damage to babies at birth would save the NHS at least an estimated £20 million a year;
- Evidence suggests that the following actions would substantially reduce risk in this area[61]:
  - improved staff supervision;
  - proper use of equipment to monitor labour;
  - better technique and diagnostic skills at delivery.

"The potential to learn from clinical negligence litigation is enormous"

4.35 A concerted effort to learn from this experience would surely prevent some future births of brain-damaged babies, reducing the misery and distress caused to children and their families and saving the NHS large amounts of money which could be diverted to other areas of patient care. This is only one example, and the potential to learn from the experience of litigation across other areas of health care is enormous.

4.36 Further evidence of the potential value of litigation information is provided by the results of a study of over 100 litigation claims paid on behalf of consultant anaesthetists working in the private sector. It found that every claim involved problems in at least one of four key areas.

Learning from litigation: Significant risk factors in anaesthesia claims

- Inadequate or no pre-operative assessment
- Failure to use essential equipment
- Medication issues, e.g. overdose of muscle relaxant
- Monitoring before, during or after the operation

Source: Medical Defence Union 1997[62]

4.37 There are currently no systematic analyses of the litigation data on hospital cases held by the NHS Litigation Authority. In primary care the medical defence organisations such as the Medical Defence Union and Medical Protection Society (which provide cover against negligence for individual practitioners in primary care and in private practice) maintain their own databases of claims and publish illustrative case-histories as an aid to learning among their members. This information can be used to identify specific trends in the nature of negligence claims in general medical practice.

Adverse incidents resulting in litgation claims in General Medical Practice

Delays in diagnosis, principally	55% of claims*
– missed malignancies	
– missed heart attacks	
– missed conditions requiring surgery	
– missed meningitis and pneumonia	
Medication errors	25% of claims
Management of pregnancy	10% of claims
Other procedures and interventions	20% of claims

* Approximate percentage of total indemnity paid out. Total value of payments in the latest 2 year period is £16.9 million.

Source: Medical Defence Union

4.38 From a more detailed examination of the area of medication errors, which account for around 25% of all litigation claims in general practice, it is possible to identify a number of recurrent problems or types of error.

Common medication errors resulting in litigation claims

- Incorrect or inappropriate dosage
- Wrong drug
- Administration error (correct medication wrongly administered)
- Contra-indicated medication (e.g. patient given medication which reacts badly with another drug or condition)
- Prescribing and dispensing errors (e.g. prescribing or dispensing an incorrect drug with a similar name to the intended medication)
- Failure to monitor progress
- Failure to warn of side-effects
- Repeat prescribing without proper checks
- Over-reliance on computerised prescribing
- Prescribing unlicensed drugs

Source: Derived from Medical Protection Society and Medical Defence Union

---

4.39 In relation to those aspects of clinical litigation relevant to our work, we drew the following conclusions:

- Clinical data arising from negligence claims are not in general being used effectively to learn from failures in care:

- There is significant potential to extract valuable learning by focusing, specialty by specialty, on the main areas of practice which have resulted in litigation.

Wasted and lost opportunities for learning from litigation in the NHS

To date little or no systematic learning across the NHS has taken place from:

- A historical base of over 14,000 claims (relating to events stretching back many years) held by the NHS Litigation Authority

- An annual rate of around 800 new claims settled by the NHS Litigation Authority arising from incidents in NHS Trusts

- A historical base of tens of thousands of claims from primary and secondary care held by organisations such as the Medical Defence Union and the Medical Protection Society*

- An annual rate of around 700 new claims settled by the medical defence organisations arising mainly from incidents in primary care*

* The MDU and MPS publish analyses of their data for the benefit of their members and have made it clear that they are willing to share information and experience to maximise the opportunities for collective learning.

Confidential inquiries

4.40 Four National Confidential Inquiries operate in the NHS:

- the **Confidential Enquiry into Maternal Deaths** (deaths of women during pregnancy or within one year of childbirth)

- the **Confidential Enquiry into Stillbirths and Deaths in Infancy** (CESDI) (stillbirths and infant deaths)

- the **Confidential Enquiry into Peri-Operative Deaths** (NCEPOD) (hospital deaths within 30 days of surgery)

- the **Confidential Inquiry into Suicides and Homicides by People with Mental Illness** (suicides within one year of contact with mental health services and homicides involving people who have been in contact with mental health services at any time)

4.41 Each Inquiry takes anonymised information, on a comprehensive or sample basis, about deaths related to a particular condition or aspect of health care and analyses it to produce recommendations for improved practice. Because of the confidential nature of the data gathering process – information is anonymised on receipt – the Confidential Inquiries are only exceptionally able to give specific feedback to individual services. Rather they publish national reports drawing on the range of events they have examined.

Key features of the confidential enquiries

- Aim to identify all deaths in a specific category
- Confidential reporting (i.e. patient, staff and hospital not identified in reports)
- Multidisciplinary review of deaths to discover avoidable factors
- Results published in periodic reports
- Key themes identified and recommendations made for improvement
- No mandatory compliance with recommendations
- No systematic monitoring of uptake of recommendations

4.42 Anonymity is widely seen as a prerequisite both for high reporting rates and for honest reporting of information about individual cases, though the experience of the Confidential Inquiries in general suggests that there are limits to the coverage which can be achieved by voluntary reporting systems. For example, the National Confidential Inquiry into Suicide and Homicide by People with Mental Illness achieved reporting rates of only around 15% for suicide until it was redesigned to draw on other sources of information – District Directors of Public Health and Office for National Statistics (ONS) data – for the initial identification of relevant incidents. Clinical information is now collected on 92% of relevant suicides and 93% of relevant homicides. The participation rate in NCEPOD, the biggest Confidential Inquiry, varied between 71% and 86% (depending on specialty) in the most recent year of study.

"it is usually left to individual services to pick up and implement specific recommendations of the Confidential Inquiries"

4.43 As discussed in paragraph 3.37 it is usually left to individual services to pick up and implement specific recommendations of the Confidential Inquiries, and there is little by way of systematic monitoring of uptake. Some recommendations have resulted in service improvements but others are repeated from report to report without action being taken. The latter are not so much those which have resource implications as those which would involve marked changes in patterns of clinical practice, and those aimed at clinicians outside the normal readership of the report. For example, the Confidential Enquiry into Maternal Deaths makes recommendations which affect general practice, accident and emergency departments and general medicine, but the reports may not be widely read by health professionals in these areas of practice.

Other external reviews

4.44 A number of bodies are active in externally reviewing aspects of NHS service provision.

Other external reviews

The Audit Commission conducts "Value for Money" studies in the NHS. These reviews are concerned with service quality, but they tend to focus on the generality – for example on "sub-optimal" care – rather than adverse incidents *per se*;

The professional regulatory bodies, such as the General Medical Council, deal with issues of individual professional performance. The drive towards proactive assessments or "revalidation" in medicine may ultimately provide a further mechanism for identifying actual or potential adverse events;

Medical Royal College visits can from time to time highlight concerns about the quality and safety of care provided in a particular unit;

The Commission for Health Improvement will have a key role both in the detection of poor quality systems, through its reviews of local clinical governance arrangements, and in the scrutiny of specific adverse incidents through its "troubleshooting" work. It also has a potentially valuable role to play in improving the conduct of NHS incident inquiries (see below) and in helping to make greater sense of the existing patchwork of external reviews.

Public Interest Disclosure

4.45 Organisational and team cultures which prevail in much of the NHS can act to discourage reporting of incidents or concerns, particularly when these relate to activities involving professional colleagues.

"The fear of being labelled a trouble-maker, the fear of appearing disloyal and the fear of victimisation by managers and colleagues are powerful disincentives against speaking up about genuine concerns staff have about criminal activity, failure to comply with a legal duty, miscarriages of justice, danger to health and safety of the environment, and the cover up of any of these in the workplace"

[HSC 1999/198 The Public Interest Disclosure Act 1998 – Whistleblowing in the NHS NHS Executive, August 1999]

4.46 Cultural barriers will take time to break down, but the Public Interest Disclosure Act 1998 (which became law in July 1999) represents an important step forward in encouraging and protecting appropriate reporting of incidents or concerns. The Act gives significant statutory protection to employees who disclose information reasonably and responsibly in the public interest and are victimised as a result, and has prompted a renewed drive to encourage open reporting in the NHS.

NHS executive guidance on "whistleblowing"

"Every NHS trust and Health Authority should:-
Have in place local policies and procedures which comply with the provisions of the Public Interest Disclosure Act 1998. The minimum requirements of local policies should include:-

(i) the designation of a senior manager or non-Executive Director with specific responsibility for addressing concerns raised in confidence which need to be handled outside the usual line management chain;

(ii) guidance to help staff who have concerns about malpractice to do so reasonably and responsibly with the right people;

(iii) a clear commitment that staff concerns will be taken seriously, and investigated;

(iv) an unequivocal guarantee that staff who raise concerns responsibly and reasonably will be protected against victimisation."

[HSC 1999/198 The Public Interest Disclosure Act 1998 – Whistleblowing in the NHS NHS Executive, August 1999]

4.47 It is too early to assess the impact of these developments. Legislative changes are not in themselves sufficient to bring about more open, learning cultures within NHS organisations, but they certainly have the potential to contribute to that process. In one sense, 'whistleblowing' can be seen as evidence of a failure to learn – people are far more likely to pursue channels outside their own organisation if there has been a failure to act on or even acknowledge concerns raised internally. To many a perceived need for external whistleblowing is in itself a sign that organisational culture is seriously awry.

Inquiries

4.48 Although they are not a mechanism for systematic information gathering, inquiries of one kind or another are an area in which the NHS invests considerable resources in an effort to learn from failures.

4.49 An inquiry can be established into a failure in the standards of care provided in a number of ways:

● An inquiry with statutory powers (e.g. to require information) ordered by the Secretary of State for Health under the powers set out in section 84 the NHS Act 1977. This tends to be for very serious issues. A recent example is the Bristol Royal Infirmary Inquiry into the deaths of a number of children following heart surgery.

- An external inquiry without statutory powers organised by the NHS locally, possibly at the request of and/or under the supervision of the NHS Executive Headquarters or one of its Regional Offices. The Secretary of State has statutory powers to set up such inquiries under his general powers in section 2(b) of the 1977 Act, as do Health Authorities to whom this power has been delegated. Two recent examples of inquiries instigated by the Secretary of State are the enquiry into the retention of children's organs after post-mortem at Alder Hey hospital and the enquiry into the case of Dr Harold Shipman, the general practitioner convicted of murdering 15 of his patients.

- A mental health inquiry established under the terms of the 1994 circular *Guidance on the discharge of mentally disordered people and their continuing care in the community (HSG(94)27/LASSL(94)4)*. These inquiries deal with serious incidents – in particular homicides – involving people in contact with mental health services.

- An internal inquiry (with or without external advisers) – this is used in the majority of serious incidents within the NHS.

"There has been little formal evaluation of these processes of inquiry"

4.50 There has been little formal evaluation of these processes of inquiry to see what impact they have. Anecdotally, there is an impression of variable focus, different levels of rigour, differences in methodology and in the way that recommendations are framed and adopted. There are no clear thresholds for determining when an inquiry should take place and what kind of inquiry is most appropriate.

NHS inquiries into adverse events: Key issues

- Thresholds for initiating an enquiry are unclear.
- Purely internal enquiries often do not reassure public.
- The NHS has variable expertise in conducting enquiries.
- There is often a long wait for the outcome.
- Written reports are of variable quality.
- Too often recommendations are not written in a format which is effective in helping to bring about the change required.
- A large amount of information is often presented, which may result in overload and act as a barrier to learning.

4.51 Experience from other fields demonstrates that the NHS experience of external incident inquiries, in particular, is not unique. Even large-scale, and apparently very thorough, inquiries in other fields sometimes fail adequately to address whole chains of critical events[63] and recommendations are often not specific enough to provide a sound basis for practical action. The sheer volume of information involved can act to inhibit effective analysis and learning. Research has also shown that there is a common core of 24 broadly similar recommendations, falling into five categories, which are made time and again by inquiries – regardless of the topic under investigation. Inquiries in the NHS often make recommendations on similar issues – for example communications among health professionals or between different agencies – but again these are sometimes not formed in such a way that people understand exactly what change they are expected to make.

Categories of core recommendations common to most enquiries

- Communication: recommendations designed to improve the communication of information between individuals, departments, other organisations and in some cases with the wider general public;
- Technical: recommending the installation of physical safety precautions where they appear to be required;
- Attempted foresight: recommendations designed to forestall different problems, not necessarily directly linked with the incident in question, which could arise in the future;
- Personnel : recommendations addressing issues such as staff training, staffing levels, lack of expertise or shortfalls in supervision;
- Authority: recommendations which attempt to produce safety by demanding it – for example through new rules, orders or legislation.

Source: Toft and Reynolds 1997[64]

"In practice the primary purposes of formal external inquiries have been discipline, learning, catharsis and reassurance"

4.52 Historically, inquiries and investigations have had to serve a range of different – and sometimes incompatible – purposes. Inquiries may be used to establish the facts of a case, provide an expert or independent perspective on an incident and help to extract learning so that services can be improved and further errors avoided. But they may also serve as vehicles for demonstrating to the public and to patients or relatives that incidents are being taken seriously, to provide a reassurance that lessons will be identified and learnt and to demonstrate accountability. Researchers have suggested that in practice the primary purposes of formal external inquiries have been 'discipline, learning, catharsis and reassurance'[65].

4.53 Each of these purposes is distinct and it is easy to see how they might come into conflict. For example, for a major incident an inquiry held in public might be more effective in assuaging public concerns and demonstrating openness, but it can be argued that public proceedings can encourage defensiveness and hamper efforts both to get at the true facts of a case and to extract learning. And a search for individuals to 'blame' as the central purpose of an enquiry can impede proper understanding of the true, often very complex, causes of failure. For ensuring that active learning takes place within organisations, formal external inquiries may be less effective than internal service reviews or audits, but the latter have tended to be of variable quality and rigour and are often not trusted by patients as sufficiently impartial or searching.

4.54 Within the NHS, there are proposals to give the new Commission for Health Improvement a remit for overseeing and improving the way inquiries are conducted. The Commission should have a major contribution to make to improving the way the NHS learns from investigations into serious adverse events, and also help to introduce some clarity into the relationships between the various existing external review mechanisms.

Health service and public health statistics

4.55 A large amount of regular statistical information is collected both by the NHS locally and by the Department of Health. The Hospital Episode Statistics (HES) capture information on 11 million hospital episodes annually in England alone, covering admission, diagnosis, resulting operations and basic outcomes (death, discharge home and other discharge). Historically, the uses of these data have concentrated on recording and assessing activity levels and on performance including technical efficiency. Much is of variable technical quality and equally variable relevance to the quality and outcomes of the care the NHS provides. It is revealing that statisticians commissioned by the Bristol Royal Infirmary inquiry into the deaths of children following heart surgery had to undertake special statistical work on HES data in order to use it to compare the performance of different cardiothoracic services around the country.

4.56 The launch of a new NHS Performance Assessment Framework, which explicitly balances efficiency with measures designed to reflect outcomes and effectiveness, has been complemented by a Clinical Indicators initiative which aims to focus on quality by exploiting HES data by linking successive episodes to produce information on post-operative mortality and re-admissions. However, whilst this information will over time help to provide a better picture of the general quality of care provided by the NHS, it is unlikely to tell us a great deal about adverse events in the short or medium term.

Analysis of information on adverse events

4.57 We have commented in our description of the various sources of information on adverse events about the extent to which the data collected are analysed to extract learning. In summary some mechanisms, such as the Confidential

Inquiries and the Medical Devices Agency and Medicines Control Agency systems have a strong focus on the rigorous analysis of information to distil lessons for practice. However, as we have made clear, little effort is made systematically to extract lessons from some potentially important streams of information, principally those arising from complaints and litigation, or to bring together the results of the various analysis systems that are in place. Regional incident reporting systems are also highly variable in the extent to which they analyse their data to distil learning.

Acting on lessons identified

4.58 It would be quite wrong to conclude that the NHS as an organisation is incapable of learning and improving, but the evidence suggests that learning generally takes a long time and that implementation of lessons can be very patchy. We have already highlighted in case studies specific kinds of problem or incident which have recurred time after time despite the fact that they have been identified as hazards.

"Where change does occur, it can take a long time to come about"

The pace of change – The example of the National Confidential Inquiries

4.59 Where change does occur, it can take a long time to come about. Even where there is good evidence from high quality systems such as the Confidential Inquiries, the evidence is that implementation of lessons and recommendations is often a very slow process, though meaningful changes can be brought about over a period of years. The Confidential Enquiry into Maternal Deaths has helped to bring about dramatic improvements in the safety of some aspects of maternity care, but an audit of specific recommendations reveals that there are still areas in which key findings have not been universally acted upon.

Examples of the pace of learning – the Confidential Enquiry into Maternal Deaths (CEMD)

Improvement occurs over a long period of time
- The rate of direct anaesthetic deaths fell from 12.8 per million births in 1970 to 0.5 per million births by 1996, though the rate of the fall was not steady during this period;

Improvement occurs patchily
- Local protocols for the management of massive haemorrhage were recommended in the CEMD report for 1985–87. In 1994, 11% of units in England still lacked such a protocol;
- Further long-standing recommendations concern the availability of on-site blood banks and Intensive Care units. In 1994, 21% of units in

England had no on-site ITU and 12% had no on site blood bank;

Some recommended improvements are not implemented
- CEMD has repeatedly recommended the establishment of a system of regional advice and referral centres for pregnancy-induced hypertension. So far such a system has not been implemented, and hypertensive disorders remain the second most common cause of maternal deaths;
- A recurring theme of CEMD reports has been the dangers of inadequate senior supervision and problems with delegation. A report in 1995 concluded that both were still factors in a number of maternal deaths;

Improvement is not always sustained
- Deaths from haemorrhage reached their lowest point in history during 1985–87, when 10 deaths occurred. The number of deaths rose to 22 in 1988–90, partly because basic lessons were being forgotten;

Some long-standing problems remain
- In the three years 1991–93, 63 deaths occurred which involved sub-standard care. Sub-standard care was a factor in 16 of 20 deaths from hypertensive disorders, 16 of 18 early pregnancy deaths and 7 of 8 anaesthetic deaths.

Sources: Hibbard and Milner 1995[66], Drife 1997[67]

4.60 Further evidence of the ability of the Confidential Inquiries to bring about change, and of the variable pace with which that change comes about, is provided by the National Confidential Enquiry into Perioperative Deaths (NCEPOD). In its 1999 report[68], NCEPOD returned to a study of 1989 and assessed the degree of change in practice in relation to surgery and anaesthesia in children. The 1989 report stated that 'surgeons and anaesthetists should not undertake occasional paediatric practice'. Comparison between 1989 and 1997/98 data shows evidence of a number of changes in practice:

Examples of the pace of learning – The National Confidential Enquiry into Perioperative Deaths, 1989 – 1998

Meaningful improvements have occurred in paediatric surgery, but they have taken a number of years to come about and in some cases recommendations have not been universally adopted:
- The proportion of anaesthetists who did not anaesthetise infants of less than six months had increased from 16% (1989) to 58% (1997/98)

- The proportion of orthopaedic surgeons dealing with small numbers (1–9 cases per year) of infants has fallen from 41% to 19% and those dealing with 10–19 cases per year has fallen from 9% to 3%
- The proportion of anaesthetists dealing with small numbers (1–9 cases per year) of infants has fallen from 40% to 26% and those dealing with 10–19 cases per year has fallen from 22% to 7%
- The proportion of orthopaedic surgeons who do not operate on infants has increased from 39% (1989) to 74% (1997/98)
- The figures for many of the other surgical specialties show similar trends, with more specialisation in children's surgery.

4.61 In neither of these examples was there a particularly strong national drive for implementation of the Confidential Inquiry recommendations, other than that coming from the professions and the Inquiries themselves.

4.62 There is far less evidence about the systematic implementation of lessons from other information sources, but the issues and examples cited in the preceding three chapters suggest that the situation with regard to most is likely to be less favourable than for the Confidential Inquiries. Aside from the Confidential Inquiries, only the Medical Devices Agency and Medicines Control Agency systems have the facility even to report on their findings in a systematic and comprehensive way. Most of the existing systems share the weakness of the Confidential Inquiries in that follow-up and implementation of lessons is left entirely to local services or even to individual practitioners.

The situation in primary care

4.63 We have already observed that the great majority of available information and evidence on adverse events in the NHS, and in the health care sector generally, relates to hospital-based care. We have also stressed that this report and its conclusions are nevertheless of equal relevance to primary care, in particular to Primary Care Groups and Primary Care Trusts as developing organisations. The case of Dr Harold Shipman, the Lancashire General Practitioner convicted earlier this year of murdering 15 of his patients, is fortunately exceptional, yet it serves as a powerful illustration of the implications of a major deficit in the reporting of serious adverse events at source.

4.64 Some of the information sources we have highlighted do encompass primary care: for example reporting of Adverse Drug Reactions and information from complaints and litigation. In particular the medical defence associations such as the Medical Defence Union and Medical Protection Society do systematically attempt to draw out and disseminate key lessons from the negligence claims they handle, providing a resource that the secondary care sector largely lacks. However some of the most valuable sources of information, such as the Confidential Inquiries, are by their nature and focus very much secondary care orientated. Historically, NHS Executive guidance on untoward incident reporting has also been heavily focused on secondary care – largely because of a perception that this is where most serious incidents occur. Yet far more patient contacts take place every year in a primary care setting and there is still the potential for patients to be seriously harmed by failures in care.

NHS activity: Adverse event reporting is least developed in sectors where the most patients are seen

Primary care
- 251 million GP consultations
- 26 million courses of dental treatment

Community health care
- 16 million new episodes

Hospital care
- 8.6 million hospital admissions
- 11.8 million new outpatients
- 12.8 million attendances at Accident and Emergency departments

Source: Department of Health Departmental Report 2000–2001. Figures quoted are for 1998–99[69]

4.65 In addition, local risk and incident reporting systems are far less developed in primary care, though there are instances of good practice in primary care risk management. Primary care faces particular challenges in developing and maintaining effective local incident risk reporting systems, not least because it has lacked some of the organisational structures to support such systems. The development of Primary Care Groups and Primary Care Trusts provides an opportunity to effect further improvements in this area, in general medical practice at least.

4.66 There is very little evidence about the capacity of primary care organisations, down to the level of individual practices, to learn actively from failures, but the general caveats we have highlighted about lack of systematic dissemination and follow-up of lessons apply at least as strongly in primary care as they do in the hospital sector.

Chapter 4 – Conclusions

- Learning from adverse clinical events is a key component of clinical governance and will be important in delivering the Government's quality strategy for the NHS. It warrants specific attention over and above wider work to improve overall risk management in the NHS;

- Although most adverse events are not related to serious problems of poor professional performance, there must be appropriate links between systems for learning from failure and those for detecting and addressing poor performance;

- The existing mechanisms for detecting and analysing serious untoward incidents and service failures in the NHS are a patchwork of systems which, in various ways and to different extents, support NHS efforts to learn from experience. NHS systems for reporting and learning from adverse events could be greatly improved, in their coverage, consistency and immediacy;

- Mechanisms for learning from adverse events in primary care are generally less well-developed than those in the hospital sector;

- There are no generally accepted definitions to guide incident reporting;

- Levels of reporting to the different existing systems vary greatly and, outside a few specific areas, are very patchy. "Near miss" reporting is almost non-existent;

- The NHS culture is not – by and large – one which encourages reporting and analysis;

- Some sources of information which might yield valuable lessons – such as complaints and litigation data – are not systematically analysed with that end in mind. The way in which complaints and litigation are handled can also hamper effective learning;

- The conduct and added value of incident inquiries is highly variable;

- Recommendations from the Confidential Inquiries, Health Service Commissioner's reports and other sources of information and analysis are often not reliably translated into practice: the onus is on individual NHS organisations to take them up and act on them;

- In general, the NHS does not appear to learn lessons consistently or quickly from the systems that are currently available to it, though there is some good practice on which to build.

CHAPTER 5

The need for action: conclusions and recommendations

In this chapter we draw together conclusions from what we have learned from an extensive review of the adequacy of present NHS information systems to detect, report, analyse and learn from adverse events in health care service, in this country. We also distil the important lessons from our review of research and experience of this field both in the health and non-health care sectors. The present situation is far from satisfactory. The NHS is failing to learn from the things that go wrong and has no system to put this right. In the context of a major programme of modernisation now being implemented in the NHS's approach to quality assurance and quality improvement, this is a gap that needs to be closed. The NHS has an old-fashioned approach in this area compared to some other sectors. Yet the opportunity for transformation is enormous with huge resulting benefits – lives can be saved, serious harm to patients can be avoided, health organisations can become much safer places for patients and staff and in the long-term large sums of money could be released which could then be used to provide more patient care.

5.1 There are at present some major shortcomings in the ways the NHS learns from its failures. Yet there are also tremendous opportunities to bring about real improvements in care, not least the beginnings of a powerful cultural shift brought about by a renewed and sustained focus on quality. There are a number of pointers from research and from other sectors that suggest how these improvements might be brought about.

5.2 For the NHS to become an organisation that can learn effectively from failure some straightforward conditions must be fulfilled.

- First, unified mechanisms are needed for reporting and analysing examples of when things have gone wrong, with clear lines of accountability. This involves both:
  – reporting of adverse events; and
  – the monitoring and analysis of a full range of adverse event data.

- Second, a more open culture must be developed, in which errors or service failures can be admitted, reported and discussed without fear of reprisal (though this does not mean that individuals should never be held to account for their actions).

- Third, lessons must be identified, whether from adverse events or from other sources of data, active learning must take place and necessary changes must be put into practice. This process needs to be actively managed.

- Fourth, the NHS must develop a much wider appreciation of the need to 'think systems' in analysing and learning from errors, as well as in prevention (through risk management).

Key problems

5.3   Within the body of our report we have drawn a number of conclusions about the weaknesses and shortcomings of the current NHS arrangements for detecting, reporting, analysing and learning from adverse events in health care, and highlighted a number of important lessons which can be drawn from research and from experience in health care and in other sectors.

Data gathering

5.4   Whilst a number of mechanisms are in operation to gather data on things that go wrong in health care, there are several systematic weaknesses.

There is no consensus on what to report. Few of the systems are based on a simple, easily communicated definition of what it is that should be reported. Few are governed by any clear reporting protocol that all staff are aware of, understand and are trained to use.

There are different, and potentially conflicting, views on the purpose of adverse event reporting systems. Functions attributed to reporting systems include:
– spotting potential clinical negligence claims;
– identifying trends in different kinds of adverse event;
– handling media coverage;
– acting as the first stage in organisational learning.

There are no proper linkages between reporting systems. Such reporting mechanisms as do exist are not integrated and seldom interrelate to each other. The usefulness of adverse event reporting systems would be improved further if a formal mechanism to consider near misses were also integrated.

Analysis

5.5   Not only do the systems for collecting information on adverse events leave
room for improvement, but there are also shortcomings in the way
information is analysed and translated into advice and recommendations for
action.

Best use is not made of available information. With the exception of the
more specialised systems (e.g. confidential clinical enquiries, adverse drug and
device reporting systems) data are not analysed or synthesised in a way that
patterns or trends can be identified. In some cases little or no analysis is
attempted beyond local level. It is a great irony, for example, that in the past
individual health care workers have been urged to see complaints as a resource
to learn from but no systematic attempt has been made to realise the huge
potential of learning from complaints to benefit the NHS as a whole.

Analysis does not reliably take place across different systems. There is no
reliable mechanism for analysing information collected through different
reporting channels to distil common themes or lessons. At present, NHS
information on adverse events is spread across nearly 1000 different organisations. This can mean that the NHS misses out on some of the more creative
approaches to analysis which we highlight in chapter 3, and that common root
causes of different kinds of adverse event go unrecognised.

Inquiries and investigations

5.6   As we have noted, there are a number of different provisions and mechanisms
for holding internal or external inquiries into individual adverse events or into
clusters of events. Yet on the evidence we have considered such inquiries, and
in particular external inquiries, are not always effective learning tools for the
NHS.

The threshold for inquiries or investigations is unclear. There is very little
clarity about the circumstances under which some form of external investigation or inquiry is appropriate following an adverse event. The need for
specific work to address this issue for mental health inquiries has already been
recognised and specific work undertaken.

**There is no clear framework or source of advice on the conduct of investiga-
tions.** Even after a decision has been taken to conduct some form of inquiry or
investigation, there is often little by way of consistent support of expertise
available to NHS organisations or to inquiry teams in the conduct of the
process. It is reasonable to suggest that this could result in a more protracted
and costlier inquiry process, and may mean that an inquiry is less thorough or
effective than might otherwise have been the case.

Inquiry recommendations are not always sufficiently helpful or focused. No doubt partly as a consequence of the lack of advice and expertise in their conduct, the products of inquiries in the NHS – in common with those in other fields – are not always focused in a way which facilitates learning and implementation. For example, a recommendation which states that communications among professionals, or between professionals and patients, are poor (a fairly frequent theme in adverse events) and must be improved might not be very helpful because it does not provide the organisation(s) concerned with an operational change to implement.

Implementation and follow-up of recommendations is patchy. In common with other sources of learning on adverse events, follow-up work to implement the recommendations of inquiries is inconsistent. Often, inquiry recommendations have no clear status, or the quality and relevance of recommendations themselves may be in doubt.

There is no systematic mechanism for sharing more widely the learning from individual local adverse event investigations. There is powerful evidence that, time after time, inquiries and investigations identify similar or identical problems and make the same sorts of recommendations. Yet there is no system for drawing together these findings to draw out general trends or to emphasise wider priorities for action. The potential implications of inquiry reports beyond the immediate circumstances of the event in question may, therefore, not always be recognised.

Understanding adverse events

5.7   The level of understanding of the nature, causes and prevention of adverse events in the health care sector is poorly developed in comparison to many fields, for example industry and air transport.

There is little basic research into the nature, causes and prevention of adverse events in health care. Most of the scientific work has been done in contexts outside the health service. Whilst much of it is likely to be extendable to the health sector, this needs to be confirmed. Equally, where exceptions occur that are particular to the NHS, these must be identified and investigated specifically.

The concept of the 'system approach' is poorly developed. There has been rapid progress in many fields in identifying the place for 'whole system' response to adverse events. Inappropriate systems are commonly a more important contributory factor than individual failings or errors. Appropriate systems can do much to reduce the burden on individuals and the resulting risk of adverse events, and to mitigate the consequences. This approach needs to be better developed in the NHS.

Information is difficult for staff to access. NHS clinicians and other staff need to access information rapidly and conveniently in the context of busy schedules. This includes both general information on the causes of adverse events and approaches to risk minimisation, and specific information on particular hazards and pitfalls. Information systems are not yet uniformly well developed enough to deliver these requirements, inhibiting the ability of the NHS to respond positively.

Learning culture

5.8 Our review of the current position confirms that there are several key areas in which the NHS falls short of being a learning organisation at the outset.

There is too often a 'blame' culture. When things go wrong, the response is often to seek one or two individuals to blame, who may then be subject to disciplinary measures or professional censure. That is not to say that in some circumstances individuals should not be held to account, but as the predominant approach this acts as a significant deterrent to the reporting of adverse events and near misses. It also encourages serious underestimation of the extent to which problems are due not to individuals but to the systems in which they operate.

No account is taken of 'near misses'. Apart from the reporting systems run by the Medical Devices Agency and Medicines Control Agency, there is no mechanism to learn from adverse events which do not result in significant harm. The 'near miss' can provide valuable information to help prevent adverse events, and is regarded in many other sectors as an important free lesson. Moreover, research suggests that for every full-blown incident there are likely to be several hundred near-misses.

There is little culture of individual self-appraisal. The education of NHS professionals depends to a variable, but generally significant, extent on clinical apprenticeship – that is, on learning by example. This process rarely counteracts a burden of public expectation of infallibility, and may often reinforce it. Yet for the NHS to learn effectively from experience, these individuals must be able to admit that perfection is not always attained: firstly and most importantly, to themselves, and then to their fellows. Where the ability to self-appraise openly and frankly is absent, the negative effects of a 'blame culture' will be reinforced

Active learning

5.9 The NHS does not, in our experience, learn effectively and actively from failures. Too often, valid lessons are drawn from adverse events but their implementation throughout the NHS is very patchy. Active learning is mostly confined to the individual organisation in which an adverse event occurs. The

"The NHS is *par excellence* a passive learning organi- sation"

NHS is *par excellence* a passive learning organisation. A number of specific weaknesses are apparent.

Some existing systems take a long time to report. The Confidential Enquiries, for example, operate to fixed timetables and produce periodic reports based on analysis of historic data. Depending on the Inquiry concerned, it can take between one and four years for the learning from an adverse event to be reflected in an inquiry report. Arrangements for giving interim feedback are not well-developed.

Implementation of recommendations takes a long time. What evidence we have on the implementation of Confidential Inquiry recommendations shows that it can take ten or fifteen years to bring about meaningful change once an inquiry has reported. We have cited one example, of suicide by hanging among mental health inpatients, of an issue which was first highlighted nearly 30 years ago but which is still a prominent problem in the NHS.

There is little or no systematic follow-up of recommendations. The recommendations arising from most reporting systems are left to individual bodies to follow up. Often it is left to future inquiry reports to comment on failures to implement earlier recommendations.

There is a lack of clarity about priorities for improvement. NHS organisations face a range of competing priorities for action from all sorts of sources. Often there is no authoritative indication of the relative priority which should be attached to particular issues.

Insufficient effort is made to target high-risk clinical procedures or to prevent the recurrence of specific catastrophic events. Research suggests that there are some procedures or areas of activity in which the likelihood of serious errors is relatively high and/or the consequences of errors are particularly serious. For example the potential consequences of obstetric and midwifery errors are very serious in human terms, and this is reflected in their prominence in litigation. There are also any number of highly complex technical procedures in which the inherent risk of error is relatively high simply because of the number of factors at work and the physical difficulty of the procedure. Similarly, there are certain very specific kinds of adverse clinical event which have recurred on a number of occasions with devastating consequences (for example the misadministration of anti-cancer drugs by spinal injection).

The possibility of developing design solutions to specific hazards is under-explored in health care. In other sectors significant efforts are being made to design equipment and products in a way which helps to minimise potential hazards, yet despite one or two examples of good practice which demonstrate its applicability to health care this approach has not yet been applied extensively or systematically in the NHS.

5.10 Table 5.1 summarises some of the key negative characteristics of the NHS's approach to adverse events, and juxtaposes the positive characteristics we believe it needs to develop in the future.

Table 5.1 A new approach to responding to adverse events in the NHS.

Past	Future
Fear of reprisals common	Generally blame-free reporting policy
Individuals scapegoated	Individuals held to account where justified
Disparate adverse event databases	All databases co-ordinated
Staff do not always hear the outcome of an investigation	Regular feedback to front-line staff
Individual training dominant	Team-based training common
Attention focuses on individual error	Systems approach to identifying hazards and prevention
Lack of awareness of risk management	General risk management awareness training provided
Short-term fixing of problems	Emphasis on sustaining risk reduction
Manipulative use of data	Conscientious use of data
Many adverse events regarded as isolated "one-offs"	Potential for replication of similar adverse events recognised
Lessons from adverse events seen as primarily for the service or team concerned	Recognition that lessons learned may be relevant to others
Passive learning	Active learning

5.11 Figure 5.2 further illustrates what we believe are some of the crucial steps in learning from adverse events. If any one of these is fundamentally flawed, the process as a whole will not perform effectively. Our recommendations, taken as a whole, are therefore aimed at achieving sustained improvements in each of the steps in this process.

Figure 5.2
Some key steps in
learning from adverse
events

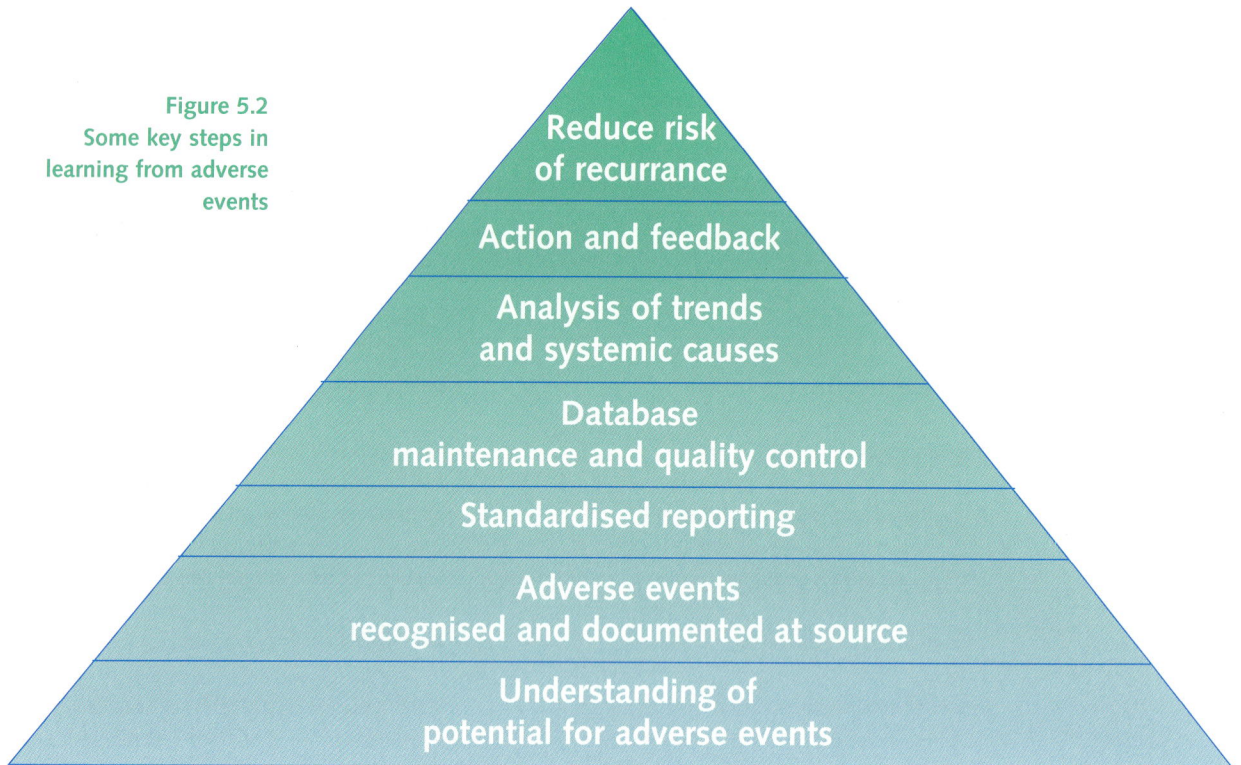

Figure 5.2 Some key steps in learning from adverse events

Reduce risk of recurrance

Action and feedback

Analysis of trends and systemic causes

Database maintenance and quality control

Standardised reporting

Adverse events recognised and documented at source

Understanding of potential for adverse events

Recommendations

5.12 Drawing on the wide range of evidence and opinion we have considered in the course of our work, we make a number of recommendations aimed at addressing the problems and weaknesses identified.

Recommendation 1: Introduce a mandatory reporting scheme for adverse health care events and specified near misses

We recommend that a scheme should be introduced by the NHS Executive to ensure comprehensive reporting of adverse events and near-misses in NHS health care settings. We recommend that this scheme should:

● be rooted in sound, standardised local reporting systems, building on and developing the current local adverse event reporting system as recommended in the NHS Executive controls assurance standard 'Risk Management System';

● adopt as the basis for reporting the concepts of an adverse health care event (AHCE) and a health care near miss (HCNM), and that these are clearly defined. As a starting point for the development of agreed definitions, we suggest;

'an adverse health care event (AHCE) is an event or omission arising during clinical care and causing physical or psychological injury to a patient';

'a health care near miss (HCNM) is a situation in which an event or omission, or a sequence of events or omissions, arising during clinical care fails to develop further, whether or not as the result of compensating action, thus preventing injury to a patient';

- operationalise these high-level definitions by developing, maintaining and making use of a set of detailed standardised categorisations of different types of adverse health care event and reportable near miss. These should be published in a standard manual detailing specific kinds of adverse event and near miss which must be reported (a) locally and (b) beyond the organisation concerned. We envisage that a 'filter' will operate so that only certain categories of event and near miss will be reported nationally or regionally. The coverage and sophistication of the categorisations should be improved over time;

- specify clearly in the manual the format in which adverse events and near misses should be reported. The reporting format and precise information to be collected should be determined only after thorough consideration of the analytical purposes to which it is to be put;

- adopt standardised computer software for adverse event and near miss reporting;

- set out clearly both the channels for reporting and the locus of responsibility for ensuring that reports are made, both within and where necessary beyond local organisations;

- be comprehensive in its coverage, incorporating all NHS organisations which deliver health care along with general practitioners and dentists treating NHS patients in primary care. The system should incorporate the arrangements for mandatory reporting of deaths in general practice announced by Health Ministers in the wake of the conviction of Dr Harold Shipman. It should also cover care provided on behalf of the NHS in private hospitals and clinics;

- be mandatory for both organisations and individuals;

- be run by an independent body which is perceived as neutral by health care staff.

Recommendation 2: Introduce a scheme for confidential reporting by staff of adverse events and near misses

We recommend that, until local reporting systems and cultures are sufficiently developed to allow all staff to feel that they can report all adverse events and near misses without fear of retribution, the national system described in Recommendation 1 should include provision for direct, confidential (but not anonymous) reporting of adverse events and near misses to regional or national level. This has been found to be of great importance in other sectors. The system should:

- be widely publicised and available to all NHS staff, as well as to family health services contractors and their employees. The viability of extending the scheme to staff in independent hospitals and clinics treating patients on behalf of the NHS should also be explored;

- have the capacity to follow-up near misses without revealing the identity of the reporter if he or she wishes. We recognise that in some circumstances it may be impossible or inappropriate to preserve anonymity – for example where there is evidence of gross negligence, criminal activity and/or a threat to patient safety and this cannot be addressed without disclosing the identity of the reporter – and this should be openly acknowledged;

- be regarded as a mechanism to be used in exceptional circumstances, with reporting channelled wherever possible through the new system described in R.1.;

- be kept under regular review as local systems and cultures develop, to determine whether continued provision of a direct confidential reporting facility, as an adjunct to the main mandatory reporting systyem (see R.1.), is both necessary and desirable.

Recommendation 3: Encourage a reporting and questioning culture in the NHS

We recommend that the NHS should encourage a reporting culture amongst its staff which is generally free of blame for the individual reporting error or mistakes, and encourage staff to look critically at their own actions and those of their teams. We acknowledge that significant progress has been made in this area in recent months and years, but believe that there is scope for further action in a number of key areas:

- NHS Trusts, Health Authorities, Primary Care Trusts and Primary Care Groups should use the implementation of clinical governance as an opportunity specifically to reinforce their procedures for adverse health care events, stressing in particular the responsibilities of all staff for reporting events and the duty of the organisation to treat individual members of staff justly, with no prior assumption of blame. General risk management awareness training for staff should be part of this process;

- local annual clinical governance reports should include explicit statements of the organisation's adverse event reporting policy, and where possible should display evidence both of real changes effected as a result of reporting and of a just approach to individuals who report their own errors;

- the provision for confidential reporting recommended in R.2. should help to give staff the confidence to report information which might otherwise go undetected;

- the NHS Executive nationally and regionally, and NHS organisations locally, should work proactively to ensure accurate media reporting of adverse events and to foster a greater public understanding of the issues involved.

- all those responsible for the initial and continuing training and education of doctors, nurses and other clinicians should address the development of an approach to frank self-appraisal. This will involve exposing clinicians to the appropriate culture of blame-free assessment and learning at every level, from undergraduate through postgraduate training to life-long learning.

Recommendation 4: Introduce a single overall system for analysing and disseminating lessons from adverse health care events and near misses

We recommend that a single overall system should be devised for analysing and disseminating lessons from adverse health care events and near misses. This system should:

- receive reports of agreed categories of events notified through the mechanisms described in R.1. and R.2.;

- analyse them in such a way that common factors and causes can be identified;

- consider and specify the action necessary to reduce risks to future patients throughout the NHS;

- ensure that feedback is provided in a way which encourages continued reporting;

- be managed or overseen by a single organisation.

Recommendation 5: Make better use of existing sources of information on adverse events

We recommend that, to facilitate fuller and more effective use of information from existing sources of information on adverse health care events:

- the new analysis and dissemination system recommended in R.4. should incorporate information and identified trends from the NHS complaints system, from litigation activity and from other reporting and analysis systems to ensure that maximum cumulative learning is extracted from these resources;

- the NHS Executive should use the opportunity provided by the forthcoming report of its complaints system evaluation to examine ways in which greater use of patient complaints as a learning resource could be encouraged and facilitated, both locally and nationally;

- the NHS Litigation Authority should work with the medical defence organisations to ensure that maximum learning is drawn from analyses of the extensive information available on clinical negligence litigation. This learning should in turn be fed into the new overall analysis and dissemination proposed at R.4.;

- patient and carer input, which can be of tremendous value in learning from adverse events, should be actively sought at each stage of the process. Systematic efforts should be made to involve patients and carers in work to implement the recommendations of this report.

Recommendation 6: Improve the quality and relevance of NHS adverse event investigations and inquiries

We recommend that the NHS Executive should work with the Commission for Health Improvement to improve the quality and relevance of adverse event investigations and inquiries in the NHS. In particular, the NHS Executive should:

- clarify the arrangements for local adverse event handling (including reporting – see R.2.), and offer further guidance to the NHS on the thresholds for different types of response, including inquiries;

- ensure that the Commission for Health Improvement as an early priority in its work programme, develops a national role in advising on process and conduct issues with the aim of ensuring higher quality and greater standardisation of inquiry conduct. Its advice should cover the framing of recommendations so that they are of maximum help to the organisation(s) concerned, and where appropriate to the NHS as a whole, in effecting practical change;

- ensure that inquiry recommendations and findings are wherever possible fed into to the proposed national adverse event reporting scheme and the associated database.

Recommendation 7: Undertake a programme of basic research into adverse health care events in the NHS

We recommend that a programme of basic research into adverse events in the NHS be commissioned by the Research Council and the NHS R&D programme. Specific foci of this programme should include:

- the incidence, nature and causation of health care adverse events;

- the extent to which knowledge from other fields is transferable to the health sector;

- practical approaches to risk minimisation and the takeup of learning; and

- the contribution of system approaches in health care;

- the use of automated methods to monitor and evaluate the performance of clinical interventions (the creation of a clinical 'black box').

Recommendation 8: Make full use of new NHS information systems to help staff access learning from adverse health care events and near misses

As NHS information systems, such as the new National Electronic Library for health, are developed to bring more rapid and convenient access to clinical and other staff, we recommend that priority is given to including access to information needed in this area. The aim should be to:

- increase knowledge on the processes of learning from experience and risk minimisation;

- include systematic information on particular causes of adverse events and how to avoid their repetition;

- present information in ways which are accessible to busy health professionals and managers;

- tailor messages and routes of communication to the needs of specific audiences; and

- maximise the contribution that improvements in information systems (such as the introduction of the Electronic Patient Record, the development of electronic prescribing systems and easy access to up to date guidelines and protocols) can make to active learning and the prevention of adverse events.

Recommendation 9: Act to ensure that important lessons are implemented quickly and consistently

We recommend that specific action is taken by the NHS Executive, the National Institute for Clinical Excellence and the Commission for Health Improvement to ensure that that important lessons from failures are quickly and reliably acted on in the NHS and that improvement is sustained. In particular, we recommend that:

- the NHS Executive should offer greater support to the NHS in prioritising actions arising from learning on adverse events. There should be a single focus within the NHS Executive for making these decisions and for ensuring that implementation is driven forward. Where appropriate, resource considerations should be taken into account when determining implementation priorities;

- the importance of implementing key lessons from adverse events, including specifically the recommendations of the Confidential Inquiries, should be given greater weight nationally by the NHS Executive as a core component of clinical governance;

- the NHS Executive should give urgent consideration to the role which routine performance management should play in ensuring that key findings from adverse event analysis are disseminated and acted upon by NHS bodies as a part of their wider clinical governance responsibilities;

- the National Institute for Clinical Excellence (NICE), as the body which now has responsibility for the operation of the Confidential Inquiries, should explore with the Chairmen and Directors of those Inquiries the possibility of developing 'fast track' processes to allow them to generate specific recommendations outside the normal reporting cycle if sufficiently serious issues emerge. We recommend that NICE should also explore with the Inquiries the options for enabling them to give more systematic feedback to individual units if a serious ongoing threat to patient safety is identified, provided this does not compromise the confidential nature of the process;

- in developing its review and reporting process for clinical governance, the Commission for Health Improvement should make provision to comment specifically on the uptake of recommendations arising from adverse event analysis and provide feedback to the relevant reporting and analysis systems to inform future work;

- both the NHS Executive and the Commission for Health Improvement should remain alert for evidence that improvement is not being sustained or that progress is slipping back, so that interventions can be planned if necessary.

Recommendation 10: Identify and address specific categories of serious recurring adverse health care event.

We recommend that there should be an explicit focus on identifying and addressing very specific serious categories of recurring serious adverse event. We recommend that as part of this work:

- the NHS Litigation Authority should be given a stronger educational remit, to work with professional bodies and the medical defence organisations to publicise high-risk areas and risk-reduction activities among managers and clinicians;

- steps should be taken to ensure better use of existing information on areas of practice and individual procedures which pose relatively high risks, in frequency of error and / or the consequences of error. Consideration should be given to the production and piloting of standardised procedural manuals and safety bulletins which it is obligatory to use when embarking on specific high-risk procedures. This work might be co-ordinated by the National Institute for Clinical Excellence;

- the NHS Executive and the Medical Devices Agency should consider how the more systematic application of design solutions could be encouraged as one means of minimising specific hazards;

- the Department of Health should establish groups to work urgently to achieve four specific aims:

  - by 2001, reduce to zero the number of patients dying or being paralysed by maladministered spinal injections (at least 13 such cases have occurred in the last 15 years);

  - by 2005, reduce by 25% the number of instances of negligent harm in the field of obstetrics and gynaecology which result in litigation (currently these account for over 50% of the annual NHS litigation bill);

  - by 2005, reduce by 40% the number of serious errors in the use of prescribed drugs (currently these account for 20% of all clinical negligence litigation);

  - by 2005, reduce to zero the number of suicides by mental health inpatients as a result of hanging from non-collapsible bed or shower curtain rails on wards (currently hanging from these structures is the commonest method of suicide on mental health inpatient wards).

Sound baselines will first need to be established for the second and third of these areas in particular, and it is important to recognise that in the short-term the number of recorded events may rise as reporting and recording systems improve.

ANNEX A

Membership of the Expert Committee on Learning from Experience in the NHS

Professor Liam Donaldson	Chief Medical Officer (Chairman)
Professor Louis Appleby	Professor of Psychiatry, School of Psychiatry and Behavioural Science, University of Manchester
Dr Jonathan Boyce	Director of Health Studies, Audit Commission
Mr Michael Buckley	Health Service Commissioner
Professor James Drife	Professor of Obstetrics and Gynaecology, University of Leeds
Professor Jenny Firth-Cozens	Director for the Centre of Clinical Psychology Research, University of Northumbria
Mrs Patricia Hart	Director of Nursing and Patient Services, Oxford Radcliffe Hospital
Dr Bill Kirkup	Regional Director for Public Health, NHS Executive Northern and Yorkshire Region
Professor Marc de Leval	Professor of Cardiothoracic Surgery, Great Ormond Street Hospital for Children
Dr Nick Naftalin	Medical Director, Leicester Royal Infirmary NHS Trust
Professor James Reason	University of Manchester Department of Psychology
Ms Marianne Rigge	College of Health
Mr Ken Smart	Chief Inspector of Air Accidents, Air Accident Investigation Branch, Department of Environment, Transport and the Regions
Professor Denis Smith	Professor of Management and Head of the Centre for Risk and Crisis Management, University of Sheffield
Professor Brian Toft	Director, Marsh Risk Consulting, Marsh UK Ltd.
Dr Charles Vincent	Reader in Psychology, University College London
Mr Steve Walker	Chief Executive, NHS Litigation Authority
Mr John Llewellyn Williams	Chairman, National Confidential Enquiry into Peri-Operative Deaths
Mr Bill Worth	Chief Executive, North Durham Healthcare NHS Trust

Secretary to the Expert Committee: Mr Simon Reeve, NHS Executive Quality Management Team

REFERENCES

Glossary

1 Ed. Kohn, L. Corrigan, J and Donaldson, M. *To Err is Human: Building a Safer Health System*. Institute of Medicine. Washington D.C. 1999
2 *The Five Steps to Risk Assessment*. Health and Safety Executive. 1998
3 Ed. Kohn, L. *et. al.* 1999 *(op. cit.)*

Chapter 1

4 *The new NHS: Modern, Dependable*. Department of Health 1997
5 *A First Class Service: Quality in the new NHS*. Department of Health 1998
6 Scally, G and Donaldson, LJ 'Clinical governance and the drive for quality improvement in the new NHS in England'. *BMJ* 1998; 317: 61–65.
7 *Supporting Doctors, Protecting Patients:* Department of Health 1999
8 *NHS Summary Accounts 1998/99*. National Audit Office 2000
9 *Handling complaints: monitoring the NHS complaints procedures (England, Financial Year 1998–99)*. Department of Health 2000
10 Source: Medical Devices Agency
11 *The Management and Control of Hospital Acquired Infection in Acute NHS Trusts in England*. National Audit Office. 2000

Chapter 2

12 Brennan,T.A. Leape, L.L. Laird, N.M. 'Incidence of adverse events and negligence in hospitalised patients'. *New England J Med* 1991; **324(6)**: 370–376
13 Leape, L.L. Brennan, T.A. Laird, N.M. *et al.* 'Incidence of adverse events and negligence in hospitalized patients: results of the Harvard Medical Practice Study II'. *New England J Med* 1991; **324**: 377–384
14 Wilson, R.M. Runciman, W.B. Gibberd, R.W. *et al.*: 'The Quality in Australian Health Care Study'. *Med J Aust* 1995; **163:4**: 58–471
15 Vincent, C.A. Presentation at BMJ conference 'Reducing Error in Medicine;. London. March 2000
16 Robbins, G. *et al.* Accidental intrathecal injection of vindesine;. *BMJ* 1985; **291**: 1094.

17 Cousins, D.H. Upton, D.R. 'Chemotherapy errors can kill'. *Hosp Pharm Prac* 1994; July/August:311–2.

18 'Doctors cleared of killing boy, 12, in cancer jab mix-up'. *Daily Telegraph*, 6 January 1999.

19 'Fatal error by hospital has claimed lives before'. *Guardian*, 6 January 1999.

20 Vincent, C.A. Young, M. Philips, A. 'Why do people sue doctors? A study of patients and their relatives taking legal action'. *Lancet* 1994; **343**: 1609–13

21 Vincent, C.A. 'Risk, safety and the dark side of quality'. *BMJ* 1997; **314**: 1775–6

Chapter 3

22 Ed. Kohn, L. *et. al.* 1999 *(op. cit.)*

23 Smith, D and Elliot D. *Moving Beyond Denial: Exploring the Barriers to Learning from Crisis.* Sheffield University 1999

24 Toft, B. and Reynolds S. *Learning from Disasters, a Management Approach* (Second Edition). Perpetuity Press. Leicester. 1997

25 Turner, B.A. and Pigeon, N.F. *Man-Made Disasters* (2nd Edition). London 1997

26 Reason, J. *Human Error.* Cambridge University Press 1990

27 Reason, J. *Managing the Risks of Organisational Accidents.* Ashgate. Aldershot 1997

28 Smith, D. *On a wing and a prayer? Exploring the human components of technological failure.* Systems Research and Behavioural Science. (in press)

29 Vincent, C. Taylor-Adams, S. Stanhope, N. 'Framework for analysing risk and safety in clinical medicine'. **BMJ** 1998; **316**: 1154–7

30 Leape, L. 'The Preventability of Medical Injury' in Bogner, M. S. (ed.) *Human Error in Medicine.* New Jersey 1994.

31 de Leval, M. Carthey, J. Wright, D. Farewell, V Reason, J. 'Human factors and cardiac surgery: a multicentre study'. *J Thorac Cardiovasc Surg* (2000 – in press)

32 Silber, J. Rosenbaum, P. Scwartz, J. Ross, R. Williams, S. 'Evaluation of the complication rate as a measure of care in coronary artery bypass graft surgery'. *JAMA* **274**: 317–323 (1995)

33 Weicke, K.E. *Sense-making in organisations.* Thousand Oaks CA. Sage Publications. 1995

34 Toft, B. 'The Failure of Hindsight'. *Disaster Prevention and Management* Vol. 1, No. 3. 1992

35 Toft, B. and Reynolds, S. 1997 *(op. cit.)*

36 Farberow, N.L. *et. al.* 'An eight-year study of hospital suicide's. *Life threatening behaviour*, 1: 184–202

37 *Safer Services – Report of the National Confidential Inquiry into Suicides and Homicides by People with Mental Illness.* London 1999

38 Toft, B and Reynolds, S 1997 *(op. cit.)*

39 Smith, D Elliot D. *(op. cit.)*

40 Firth-Cozens, J. 'Teams, Culture and Managing Risk' in Vincent, C (ed.) *Clinical Risk Management.* BMJ Books. London 2000

41 Wason, P. 'On the failure to eliminate hypotheses in a conceptual task'.

Quarterly Journal of Experimental Psychology Vol. XII 1960 Part 3.

42 Reason, J. 1997 *(op. cit.)*

43 Reason, J. 1997 *(op. cit.)*

44 The Pennington Group report on the circumstances leading to the 1996 outbreak of infection with E.coli O157 in Central Scotland, the implications for food safety and the lessons to be learned. The Stationery Office, Edinburgh 1997

45 Sheriff Nigel Morrison QC. *Determination in Inquiry into the circumstances of the death of Darren Denholm.* Sheriffdon of Lothiam and Borders at Edinburgh. February 2000

46 Toft B. 'Modifying Safety Culture: An Empirical Perspective (Part 2'). *Risk management Bulletin* Vol. 2, Issue 6, Feb 1998

47 Heinrich HW, *Industrial Accident Prevention: A Scientific Approach.* New York and London 1941

48 Toft, B. 1992 *(op. cit.)*

49 Toft, B. 1992 *(op. cit.)*

50 Turner, B.A. and Pigeon, N.F. 1997 *(op. cit.)*

51 Toft, B. *Personal communication* 1999

52 Sir Cecil Clothier (Chairman). The Allitt Inquiry. HMSO, London 1994.

53 Toft, B. *Personal communication* 1999

54 Toft, B. *Personal communication* 1999

55 Toft, B and Reynolds, S. 1997 *(op. cit.)*

56 John Main QC (Chair). *Report of the Independent Team Inquiry into the Care and Treatment of NG.* Ealing, Hammersmith and Hounslow Health Authority 1996. Summarised in Reith, M. 'Community Care Tragedies: a practice guide to mental health inquiries'. *British Association of Social Workers.* Venture Press 1998

57 Toft, B. *Personal communication* 1999

Chapter 4

58 Department of Health 1999 *(op. cit.)*

59 Dineen, M. and Walsh, K. 'Incident reporting in the NHS'. *Health Care Risk Report* March 1999

60 Department of Health 2000 *(op. cit.)*

61 Ennis, E. and Vincent, C. 'Obstetric accidents: a review of 64 cases'. *BMJ* 1990; 300: 1365–1367

62 Medical Defence Union Risk Management Services, *Risk Management on Anaesthesia.* 1997

63 Toft, B. Turner, B.A. 'The Schematic Report Analysis Diagram: a simple aid to learning from large-scale failures'. *International CIS Journal* Volume I(2) April/May 1987

64 Toft, B. and Reynolds, S. 1997 *(op.cit.)*

65 Reder, P. and Duncan, S. 'Reflections on Child Abuse Inquiriues' in Peay, J. (ed.) *Inquiries After Homicide.* Duckworth. London 1996

66 Hibbard, B. and Milner, D. 'Auditing the audit – the way forward for the Confidential Enquiries into Maternal Deaths in the United Kingdom.' Contemp. Rev. *Obstet. Gynaecol.*, 1995, Vol 7, April 1995.

67 Drife, J.O. 'Lessons to be learnt from maternal mortality reports'. *Current Obstetrics & Gynaecology* (1997)7, 218–223

68 *The Report of the National Confidential Enquiry into Perioperative Deaths 1997/1998.* London 1999

69 *Department of Health – The Government's Expenditure Plans 2000–2001.* The Stationery Office, London. 2000.